DEADLY SECRET

DEADLY SECRET

JENNIFER LYNN

PURGING INNER DEMONS

Tate Publishing & Enterprises

Published by Tate Publishing & Enterprises, LLC
127 E. Trade Center Terrace | Mustang, Oklahoma 73064 USA
1.888.361.9473 | www.tatepublishing.com

Tate Publishing is committed to excellence in the publishing industry. The company reflects the philosophy established by the founders, based on Psalms 68:11,
    "The Lord gave the word and great was the company of those who published it."

Book design copyright © 2007 by Tate Publishing, LLC. All rights reserved.
Cover design by Liz Mason
Interior design by Sarah Leis

Published in the United States of America

ISBN: 978-1-60247-425-3

07.05.11

I lovingly dedicate this book to my family, friends, and medical professionals who have helped me through my tough journey with bulimia nervosa. A special thanks to the one I opened my heart to through prayer. Thank you, Lord, for listening and giving me the strength.

ACKNOWLEDGMENTS

I would like to express my appreciation to the many friends and family I have been blessed to encounter along life's journey. I wish I could name every person who has made a difference in my life, but this would be impossible.

A special thanks to the following:

David, Colby, Shanon, and Zachary—They have shown me the wonders of loving unconditionally and how to laugh at myself and life. God has truly blessed me with a wonderful family.

Mom—My mother has given me many wonderful qualities such as the love of music, teaching, books, and children. I am truly blessed to have a mother as talented and loving as mine.

Dad—My father has taught me how to have fun in life, and to see the beauty and peace in God's miraculous creation of nature. Thank you for the many memorable walks in Bluff Woods.

Kimberly—She has taught me to be more outspoken. It is okay to have my own opinion and voice.

Christopher—He has taught me to be compassionate of people with special needs.

Grandma and Pa McCracken/Grandma and Pa Tapscott—Thank you for supporting me in my journey of writing this novel. Your love and acceptance of who I have become means more to me than words can express.

Patrick Dooley—My love for you has only grown stronger over the years. I believe there is a reason God chose you to be my best friend. Our unique friendship, the love we shared, and our long talks will forever be alive in my heart.

Laurie, Caroline, and Phil—I am convinced the Lord has brought these special friends into my life so I could understand how to have a relationship with Him. They have taught me to trust in the Lord and to be forgiving of others and myself.

Melanie and Kristen—Thank you for your support and friendship, especially the challenging teenage years.

Steve Smith—Thanks for helping me reach people through the web.

Trinity Episcopal Church—The support and words of encouragement from church friends is much appreciated. A special thanks to Father Hartjen and Father Harris for their spiritual guidance.

TABLE OF CONTENTS

PREFACE

This story comes from personal experiences in my life. At one time these experiences were secretive and very painful to talk about. I have spent many years talking with therapists and listening to others stories in hopes of better understanding my illness. With help from the Lord, I can honestly say that I am able to talk about my experience now without feeling shame and embarrassment.

When I was actively practicing bulimia nervosa, I felt I would never be able to stop this behavior. It was a part of me just like my arms and legs are a part of me. I had literally hit rock bottom and didn't think I would survive. Amazingly, I am still here today to tell my story.

As I wrote my story, there were times when tears started to fall. All of the hurt and pain from the past flooded my emotions. As I continued to write, I discovered how God's plan for my life was revealed step by step throughout my youthful years.

Recovering from an eating disorder was not easy and many tears have been shed. I did not feel like I was worthy of life and love of others. It took a lot of support from family, friends, and medical professionals to help attain better self-esteem to overcome this powerful and very dangerous illness. The pain that I have endured has made me a stronger and more compassionate person. All of my life experiences, good and bad, have made me the person I am today.

My goal is to share my experience of having an eating disorder through this story and to give you hope in your daily struggles and life's journey. If I can reach one individual through this story and help them from ever starting an eating disorder, or perhaps someone who is actively practicing to overcome that eating disorder, then I have accomplished my goal. Education and awareness are powerful tools in preventing illnesses from ever starting. Once you have an eating disorder, it is extremely difficult to overcome and is a lifelong struggle.

I have learned through experience that pain is a part of life, but suffering can be optional. You may suffer temporarily, but there is light at the end of the tunnel.

Several names of people in the story have been changed. This story is not intended to set blame on others for my illness. I do not want attention focused on individuals involved in my life, but rather the lesson to be learned.

I pray this book will bring glory to God, and will be spiritually uplifting to each person who reads it.

INTRODUCTION

Courteney stepped out into the cool air of a beautiful autumn morning. This was her favorite season of the year. The leaves on the trees turn the most gorgeous colors. She glanced at the tall oak in her yard and admired the beautiful fall colors of orange, yellow, and red showing through. She noticed a squirrel at the trunk collecting acorns to prepare for the long winter months ahead.

She felt the warm sensation of happiness within herself as she sat down on the porch swing. This was her favorite place to go in the early morning while her children were still sleeping. She loved living in the country where it was quiet and if you listened closely enough, you could hear the sounds of different animals. Her favorite was the rooster crowing in the early morning hours. Of course, her rooster didn't seem quite normal at times. He crowed morning, noon, and night. But the sound she loved and that's all that really mattered. A feeling of peace overcame Courteney. She longed for so many years to know that feeling.

Courteney started thinking about the day ahead of her and began feeling nervous, yet excited. Her dreams and hard work had finally paid off. She smiled and a tear trickled down her rosy cheek. She quickly brushed away the tear. She did not want to get teary eyed and emotional today. This was a day that she longed for and had worked so hard to achieve. If someone had told her twenty years ago that she was going to be a guest speaker and talk about her eating disorder, she would never have believed them. Life back then seemed so painful and hopeless.

She leaned her head back against the cushioned seat and

started to leisurely swing. It's funny how such a simple thing in life, like swinging, can make one feel better—bring such peace and relaxation. When she thought back over her younger years, she wished she had known then what she knew now. Perhaps it is only when we become mature adults that we can really understand and appreciate our younger years. There were many good times, but Courteney had her share of challenges.

Courteney had grown up in a household with very loving parents and it seemed like the perfect family. But everyone knows, no family is perfect and all families have their secrets. But as she saw it, if she hadn't had some good teachings going on in her family life, her life story might have had a more tragic ending.

Courteney was startled by a cold, wet nose on her hand. She looked down to see her spirited dog wanting attention. Sabrina loved to have her belly rubbed. She would always let you know her demands by rolling over on her back and lying on your feet. There was no getting up until she got what she wanted.

"How you doing this morning girl?" asked Courteney with a loving voice while stroking Sabrina's head gently.

She loved her rottweiler. Sabrina had proven to be a very intelligent dog and a great companion. She loved her like she was one of her own children.

Courteney settled back into the swing once again. She closed her eyes and started thinking about the day ahead of her. She needed to think about what she would say. Where should she start telling her story? Would she be able to make a difference? She needed to organize her thoughts. Her mind started taking her back in time, back to the time when she was a young teenager. It was the 1980's in a small historical town located in the bluffs along the Missouri River, in the Northeast corner of Kansas. The town was named Atchison, Kansas, and Courteney was fourteen years old. This is Courteney's story:

Atchison, Kansas 1982

I lay in bed staring at the ceiling trying to decide if I wanted to go to school that day. I could fake a migraine and it was a sure bet I'd get to stay home. I had a history of migraines and knew that my mother would believe me. The thought of having to go to school and face the hateful remarks, the hurtful gossip, and the torment that other kids inflicted on me was more than I could handle at times. I pulled the blanket up over my head, smelling the scent of fresh linens; I wished I could just stay hidden there all day.

"John. Courteney. Kelli. Time to get up."

Mom's morning call drifted into the bedroom. I needed to decide quickly what I was going to do. Then I remembered it was Friday. I had a slumber party tonight with the neighborhood girls. I really wanted to go over to Susie's house and spend the night. There was going to be four of us playing board games, talking, popping popcorn, and watching movies until hopefully the sun came up. Our goal was to stay up all night, and you didn't want to be the first to fall asleep. The first asleep gets something humorous done to her. Once they soaked my bra in water and froze it in the freezer. I always tell myself I'm not going to fall asleep, but usually I'm the first one.

I just couldn't miss out on this party. These girls were actually nice to me. It didn't bother me that they were one year younger. I was a freshman this year. I wanted to hang out with kids my own age, but for some reason I just wasn't fitting in with my class. This was my third year at this school, so it wasn't like I was the new kid anymore. What's wrong with me? Those were words that I often thought to myself.

"Courteney, are you getting up?" Mom asked with a hurried tone in her voice. Getting three children up and ready for school was not always an easy job.

"I'm getting up now, Mom."

Mom looked at me with concern. "Are you okay, Courteney? Are you feeling well today?"

"Sure Mom. I'll be out for breakfast in a minute."

Slipping out from underneath the covers, I started rushing around to get ready for school. Looking into the vanity mirror, I decided I would go with my typical hairstyle for the day. I usually put my long, sandy blonde hair in a pony tail, especially when it was hot and muggy outside. The school wasn't air conditioned and could get uncomfortable. I threw on my green cotton shorts and a t-shirt I had purchased at camp last summer. We had dance practice after school, which was usually my favorite part of the day. I loved being on the dance team and was ecstatic when I made co-captain. I had tied for captain with another girl, Lauren, so they decided to have two co-captains.

I glanced at my alarm clock and realized I only had ten minutes and we would be heading out the door for school. I couldn't make mom late. She was a teacher at our school, and I didn't want her being late for work my fault. She usually had morning hall duty. My mother, Mrs. Randi Baker, was the typing teacher. Her class was definitely my favorite and, as far as I could tell, she was liked by all the students.

"Courteney, come on. Mom wants us in the car now," Kelli said with agitation in her voice.

Kelli, my sister, is sixteen months older, but lately you'd think that she was at least ten years older. We always had our little quarrels when we were younger, but we would've always stuck up for each other. Lately we just can't get along. I keep telling myself that it has to do with going into our teenage years. You could say that we were the two sisters that are like night and day.

Kelli was very outspoken, popular, and exceptionally pretty. She had the prettiest long, brown hair and a figure all the girls envied. I was very shy, afraid of hurting others feelings, sensitive, definitely not popular, and average looking. No matter how much I exercise and diet, I just can't seem to have a figure like all the popular girls.

Running into the kitchen, I grabbed a diet soda and a granola bar out of the refrigerator for breakfast.

"Are you coming, Courteney?" Mom asked giving me a big smile.

"Sure, I'm ready."

I was correct about the school being hot and miserable. I was anxious for the cool autumn weather to settle into our small town. It made for a miserable day when you had to sit eight hours in a stuffy building listening to a teacher's lecture. School and academics were important to me, but politics was just not my thing. Listening to Mr. Cook lecture about our president, Ronald Reagan, and how our government is structured, was a lot to ask of me in this heat.

Math, science, cooking, and typing were my favorite classes. There was only one class hour left before school was dismissed, and luckily, my last hour was one of my favorite classes—typing with mom. It wasn't my favorite because of my mother being the teacher. I loved to type. I was the fastest typist in the class. I could type eighty-five words a minute with less than three mistakes.

So far I had managed to dodge the clique of girls in my class that had officially crowned themselves as queens of the school. There's nothing wrong with wanting to hang out with people you feel comfortable with, but it does become a problem when the group starts rejecting and hurting everyone that they feel isn't like them. I definitely fit into the category of people that wasn't like them.

There were four girls that were leaders, with unfortunately many followers. I'll be honest, I didn't care for them, but for some strange reason I needed their approval. I needed to have a sense of belonging in this class, yet I wanted my independence. I didn't want to follow other students just to be in their clique, especially when I disapproved of their morals and behavior towards others. I couldn't figure out why everyone just couldn't be friends. It was hard for me to be mean to someone, even when they treated me unpleasantly.

The bell for last hour rang, and I headed for my locker. I turned the corner and sure enough there stood Shelly, Cindy, Tami, and Sami Jo. They were waiting for me at my locker. There was no dodging the four queens of the school now. Smiling, I cautiously approached my locker and said, "Hi."

All four were snorting like pigs saying, "Hi Miss Piggy."

Giggles lingered through the school hallway. I wanted to get out of there as quickly as possible. I opened my locker and suddenly felt pain shoot through my hand and shoulder. They slammed my locker door on my hand and knocked me against my locker. I could feel tears burning my eyes. Being a sensitive person was not working in my favor at the moment. I knew I wouldn't be able to hold back the tears. My entire body started shaking, and I could feel the sudden sensation of being sick to your stomach.

"What's the matter, Miss Piggy?" Sami Jo asked while flipping her long blonde hair over her shoulder.

Sami Jo was a petite, blonde haired cheerleader that was always flipping her hair around like she was something special.

"Are you going to run to your mommy and tell her we're being mean again?"

Without saying a word, I slammed my locker and walked as fast as I could to last hour. Giggles and a few bad names could be heard as I was walking away.

It wasn't going to look good with me crying and walking into mom's class. Thankfully, they didn't have last hour with me and their classes were in a different direction. I knew I wouldn't have to face them again today. I'd just stay in mom's room and walk with her to dance practice. She was the coach and would be going that direction too. Those girls wouldn't dare be mean to anyone in front of a teacher or a parent. They were the type of girls who would be so nice to you in front of a teacher, and when the teacher was out of earshot they were different people. It wasn't a nice kind of different either.

I dried my eyes so my mom couldn't tell I had been crying. She knew I was having a hard time fitting in, but I purposely spared her all the details of my misery. Mom and I were close, and I did tell her some of the nasty things they did. I didn't tell her everything though. I knew it hurt my mother when I told her stories about what the girls said and did to me. I sure didn't want to hurt my mother, and I didn't want to disappoint her either. There are many times when I feel like I am a disappointment to my parents. My sister, Kelli, wasn't having all these problems. Why me?

I sat down at my typewriter and started on the warm-up. I was still shaking and needed to calm down. Closing my eyes, I took a deep breath and let it out slowly. I repeated this several times until I could feel my insides calming down.

"Hi, Courteney."

Startled, I jumped. Looking up I was glad to see a friendly face.

"Hi, Kirsten."

"Are you okay, Courteney?"

"I'm fine, thanks. Are you coming to dance practice tonight, Kirsten?"

"I'll be there," Kirsten replied with a welcoming smile.

Kirsten sat down at the typewriter in front of me and started her warm-up. Kirsten knew what it was like to be bullied by Sami Jo and the gang. She got her fair share of teasing and bullying because of her weight.

My grandmother always told me that when it comes to human beings it doesn't matter what they look like on the outside, but what matters is the kind of person they are on the inside.

Kirsten was always nice to me, and I thought of her as one of the most beautiful people I knew. She had the prettiest silky, brown hair that came just below her shoulders. She never failed to have a welcoming smile to brighten my day. We were both on the dance team and roomed together when we went to summer camps. We had a great time together, and Kirsten was a terrific dancer.

Dancing and music were my passion. They made me feel better when I was down. If it hadn't been for the dance team, I wouldn't have wanted to go to school.

I ran into the house to get ready for tonight's slumber party. I needed to get a shower after having dance practice, do my chores, and eat dinner before I could leave.

Mom always fixed my favorite on Friday nights. She melted Velveeta, Rotel, and cheese soup together to make the most wonderful dip. My favorite way to eat the cheese dip was to crush my Doritos into tiny pieces and pour the dip over them. I knew I shouldn't be eating fattening food like cheese dip, but it was so good. I would never lose weight and be accepted by Sami Jo and the gang if I didn't start eating less fattening food.

Without even asking, I knew the neighbors, Mike and Marsha, would be over to eat dinner and talk with my parents. This was a ritual on Friday nights. I used to enjoy listening to their grown-up talk and jokes. Mike was the kind of person that if the party was dead, he would bring it to life. He was loud, always told funny jokes that were on the inappropriate side, and could easily make a person laugh.

Marsha was very fashionable, silly, and made you laugh too. She owned a boutique on the downtown square. There were times during the holidays when she needed extra help and I'd get to work at the boutique. It was a lot of fun working in a clothing store, especially since I like to shop.

Unfortunately, I experienced a different side of Mike. I didn't enjoy being around him anymore.

Less than a year ago, I had gone on a camping trip with my Dad, Mike, my brother John, and a friend by the name of Leah. After retiring to bed for the evening, Mike tried to have his way with me. One minute I'm in the back of the Subaru sleeping soundly next to Leah. The next, I was awakened by a drunk, unclothed, older man trying to seduce me. I had never seen this much of a man in my life, nor did I want to. If it hadn't been for Leah, he would've had his way. We both screamed and beat on him until he left me alone. My dad was asleep in a tent about ten feet from the car. He didn't hear me scream, because he had been drinking too and was sound asleep.

I'll never forget that night. The shame and embarrassment I felt inside were hard to bear at times. Whenever I saw Mike I wanted to scream at him. Why would somebody that you were supposed to trust do something like that to a fourteen-year-old child? I knew I couldn't tell my parents what their friend had done. My father never wanted to hear anything negative. My mother had enough to handle without hearing about my problems all the time. I knew it would just hurt her.

"Courteney, can I come in?" asked John from the other side of my bedroom door.

"Sure, come on in."

"Will you play a game with me tonight?

"Not tonight, I'm going to Susie's to spend the night. Maybe tomorrow."

John looked sad as he shut the door. John is two and a half years younger than me. My heart went out to him. John had been diagnosed with autism and struggled with being accepted too.

John was an adorable blonde haired, blue eyed, loving individual. He would give everything he had to someone just to be liked. School, social acceptance, and making friends were not easy for him. He had his times when he would throw temper tantrums and then he'd turn around and be so lovable. How to help John was a puzzle to me. I couldn't even figure out how to help myself be more accepted by my peers.

Sure enough, Mike and Marsha showed up for dinner and drinks. Mike and Dad sat at the bar having their routine nightly mixed drinks while everyone else ate dinner.

Dad rarely ate dinner with the family. He usually had a small package of peanuts and washed them down with several mixed drinks. He let mom know too that she didn't need to eat much, because it might make her fat. It bothered me when I heard him saying that to her.

Mom was such a beautiful, loving person. I definitely didn't see her as heavy. We were about the same size, and at times would swap clothes. In front of us kids, Mom never showed much of a reaction to his weight comments. I often wonder how it makes her feel.

My dad, Steve, was the Chief Financial Officer of Atchison Hospital. It was a small ninety-six bed hospital with about half the beds housing Cray Manor patients. Cray Manor was a nursing home that occupied two of the floors at the hospital.

21

When I would visit dad at work, he would take me up to the Cray Manor floors to visit with the elderly. I enjoyed visiting with them. One woman I'll never fail to forget. I can't recall her name, but I do remember she was one hundred and two years old. The fact that she had reached a triple digit age was mind boggling for me. I can't imagine living so long with all the pain that I felt inside. I can't explain why I was so fascinated by this woman, but my father sensed my fondness for her. He took me to visit this elderly woman several times before she passed away.

When my father wasn't working, he sure knew how to have fun. He loved to take us hiking up Bluff Woods across the river in Missouri. The section of the bluffs that we enjoyed hiking the most was halfway between Atchison and St. Joseph, Missouri, off of fifty-nine highway. There was an area where you could build campfires and roast marshmallows and hot dogs. Usually, we built our campfire first then headed up the bluff.

My favorite part of the hike was listening to the ripples of the stream that flowed swiftly down the bluff while crossing the rickety old bridge. John and I enjoyed climbing Bluff Woods the most with him. John had more energy than a young pup and at times it was hard to stay up with him. He always made it to the top first.

I knew dad loved all of us. He was like a young kid in a grown-up body. Dad was all about having fun, but for some reason he wasn't the kind of person you could talk to when there was a problem. I often wonder why he has a difficult time with discussing and working through conflicts.

I finished my dinner and put my bowl in the sink.

"I'm leaving for Susie's house now, Mom. I'll see you in the morning," I stated grabbing my sleeping bag.

Giving me one of her warm hugs and smiles mom said, "Have fun. We'll go shopping in the morning."

I kissed her and ran out the door to head to Susie's house. Little did I know that this slumber party would change my life forever.

The Slumber Party

As I was running out the garage door, I stopped when I heard my dog whining. Looking over towards her bed, I spotted my droopy eared, brown eyed dachshund giving me this pitiful look. My heart went out to Suzy. She was getting older and needed lots of love. She would've liked to be a house dog, but my mother was allergic to animals. Animal hair made mom's allergies go wild. I was thankful that I didn't inherit mom's sensitivity to animals, because I have a huge love for them.

Occasionally, I sneak Suzy into my bedroom at night without mom knowing. Of course, sometimes I wonder if mom might know I'm bringing her into my bedroom and just not saying anything. Suzy has this uncontrollable habit of leaving short, brownish red hair everywhere she lays. I tuck her under my covers at the foot of my bed so mom won't see her. Suzy licks my toes, which would of course tickle, and I'd never find sleep this way. Suzy would eventually inch her way up into my arms and settle in for the night. If Suzy could talk, I'd be in trouble. I loved to talk to her and tell her all my secrets and dreams. She looked at me like she truly understood.

I bent down to pick her long, slender body up into my welcoming arms.

"Hi, Suzy. I love you, girl," I said giving her a gentle hug and kiss.

Suzy may not be able to talk back, but I could feel one of her warm, wet, and sloppy kisses being smeared across my face. She could always make you feel loved and needed.

23

"I'm not going to be here tonight, girl. I'll be back tomorrow, and we'll go for a walk. I love you bunches," I said while stroking her smooth, soft fur.

Giving her another kiss on the head, I laid her back on her pillow bed.

As I was turning to leave, I saw my sister pulling into the driveway. She was probably just getting home from dance practice. She is in tenth grade this year and on the high school dance team. I couldn't wait to try out for the high school team next year.

"Hi. How was practice?" I asked Kelli as she was getting out of her car.

"Fine. Where are you going?"

"I'm going to Susie's house for a slumber party. I'll be home tomorrow. Mom said she'd take us shopping," I said with excitement in my voice.

"See you tomorrow," I said waving good-bye to Kelli.

"Wait a minute," Kelli said with a hateful tone to her voice.

"You didn't take any of my clothes with you, did you? Did you get into my closet?" Kelli asked with a harsh tone and hateful expression on her face.

"No, I did not get into your possessions Kelli; I know I'm not allowed to touch your precious belongings," I stated with sarcasm in my voice.

Kelli had this juvenile rule that I was not allowed into her room under any circumstances to touch or borrow anything. She came into my room and borrowed clothes from my closet at her leisure, but I wasn't allowed to even touch her belongings.

"You better not have. If I find out you were in my room you are in trouble."

"Yes, I know, Kelli. I wouldn't dare go into your room. Bye."

I turned and ran across the street to Susie's house. My sister had this way of trying to spoil an evening that was supposed to be fun.

Susie had been watching for me and already had the door open by the time I reached her house.

"Hi, Courteney," Susie said cheerfully.

"Hi, Susie," I said smiling at her and stepping into her house.

She was such a beautiful girl and I envied her. She had long, silky blonde hair and was so petite. She reminded me of a model off the front cover of a magazine.

Tatum and Olivia were already there and busy playing Yahtzee. I plopped myself down on the front room floor next to Tatum so I could get in on the next game. A full house was the easiest for me to roll, but I rarely rolled a Yahtzee. This was one of our favorite games to play at slumber parties, and Tatum was always the lucky winner. She never failed to roll at least two Yahtzee's in every game. It didn't bother me to lose a game. I always tried to be a good sport when it came to games, knowing it was just in good fun.

"Hi, guys. Who's winning?" I asked cheerfully. They all looked at me and started giggling.

"Who do you think?" asked Olivia.

We all started laughing, because we knew who was winning. But we didn't care. We were having a good time and the evening was starting off great, that's all that mattered.

Tatum and Olivia are both on the dance team and excellent dancers. I knew that one of them would most likely be captain of the dance team their freshman year. They usually roomed together at the summer dance camp we attended every year.

Tatum has short, brown hair and the bubbliest personality. I envy her sometimes. She always seems so happy and in control of her life. She is one of the smartest people I know. Despite her good looks, great personality, her intelligence, and the fact that she is talented; she is nice. I enjoyed being around Tatum, and I knew she would always be a friend.

Tatum also lives right next door to me. Sometimes she and I will sneak out at night and walk down to the pond at the country club. Our quiet neighborhood lies on the outskirts of town on the edge of Bellevue Country Club. It is a newer housing addition, called Westridge, with about two dozen new homes.

One of the favorite things the neighborhood children enjoyed was to go down to the pond at the country club. There wasn't a lot to do at the pond but sit next to it and talk, but we enjoyed going there. I'm not sure if we enjoyed going there because of our long talks, or perhaps it was because we thought we were getting away with something we weren't supposed to be doing.

Olivia didn't live in Westridge, but she was at Susie or Tatum's house quite often. They were all in eighth grade and close friends. Olivia had pretty, brown hair that was shoulder length. She had the prettiest smile and was quite often noticed by the boys in her class.

The evening was a typical slumber party. We played Yahtzee, Monopoly, and listened to some of our favorite songs. I brought one of my favorite cassette tapes, Phil Collins, to listen to. We even played Truth or Dare. I always choose a truth over a dare, because it seemed the dares were far more embarrassing than the truth questions.

"Who wants something to eat?" asked Susie with enthusiasm in her voice.

Tatum and Olivia jumped up and cheerfully shouted, "I do!"

I followed them into the kitchen not knowing what to say. I could eat something, but I already had dinner and knew I really didn't need the extra calories. Eating something this late was sure to result in gaining weight.

I had told myself that I was going to eat smart and try to lose ten pounds. If I could just lose this unwanted weight, I would weigh one hundred ten pounds. I'd feel better about myself. I might even look more like the other girls in my class. It seems like all the other girls could eat anything they wanted, as much as they wanted, and they still stayed thin. It just wasn't fair. I look at food and seem to gain weight.

I could smell the buttery aroma of popcorn in the air. Tatum was popping popcorn and filling bowls for everyone. There was more than popcorn to eat. We had big bowls of ice cream, homemade chocolate chip cookies that Olivia's mom baked, and some leftover pizza. I felt so guilty inside and didn't know if I should eat all of this wonderful, delicious food. I wanted to, but knew I was doomed to weight gain.

I nibbled on the popcorn but was determined not to touch the other alluring foods. Olivia, Tatum, and Susie were laughing and eating like there was no tomorrow. They don't even act like they feel guilty about eating all this fattening food or worry about gaining weight. I just can't figure it out. How can they eat like this and never gain weight?

"I have to know something guys. How do you eat all of this food and still stay so petite?" I asked with curiosity. They all looked at each other with a blank look on their faces.

Tatum gently took my hand and said, "Come with me, I'll show you."

We walked down the hallway, went into the bathroom, and shut the door.

"You can't tell anyone, Courteney. This is a secret. Do you promise not to tell?"

"Yes, I promise," I responded.

She knew I would keep my word.

"You just make yourself vomit the food back up," Tatum explained like there was nothing to it.

Dumbfounded I asked, "How do you do that?"

Tatum leaned down in front of the toilet, stuck her finger down her throat and started vomiting. I couldn't believe what I was seeing. I wasn't sure what to say or do and I was starting to feel sick myself. I didn't know what to think. Was this okay to do? Did all girls do this to stay thin?

Tatum stood up, flushed the toilet, and started washing her hands and face.

She turned to face me and giving me a serious look she stated, "Don't forget, this is a secret."

"I won't forget. Your secret is safe with me."

We headed down the hallway and joined the other girls in the front room. Everyone was acting like nothing important just took place, and I couldn't tell if Susie and Olivia even knew what happened in the bathroom. For the rest of the evening, my mind was preoccupied with thoughts about what happened. I was having a hard time relaxing and enjoying the rest of the evening.

I had mixed feelings about this behavior. My gut feeling told me this was unacceptable, but I started rationalizing the behavior. People get sick with the stomach flu and other illnesses that make them vomit. This really wasn't much different. The only difference that I could see was you were just helping yourself vomit. Tatum didn't seem too effected by it afterwards. Watching her, you would never even know she had just been in the bathroom vomiting. Could this be my answer to losing weight and getting a better body like the other girls? If I could just lose ten pounds I would be accepted by Sami Jo and the gang and become more popular with my peers.

"I'm getting tired, guys. Mom is taking us shopping in the morning so I think I'll head to bed. Goodnight."

"Night, Courteney," all three responded.

I wasn't really getting tired, but I needed to be by myself. I needed to think about this behavior I had just encountered.

I curled up inside my sleeping bag and stared out the window at the moon and stars. It was a clear, beautiful evening and it seemed I could catch sight of every star in the sky. I could hear Susie, Olivia, and Tatum in the other room giggling and listening to music.

I started to recall what my grandmother had always said, "What the person is like on the inside is far more important than their appearance on the outside."

Was grandma correct? I wasn't sure. I was a good person on the inside and tried to be kind to everyone regardless if they had a handicap, had a different skin color, or were less fortunate than our family. I definitely had a good inside, but yet I was made fun of, called bad names, and treated awfully by others.

Even my sister, who I love and was supposed to trust, wasn't always the nicest to me. I was different than her, but yet everybody seemed to compare us and expected me to be more like her. It wasn't uncommon for her to have straight A's on her report card. I might have a few A's, a couple B's, and an occasional C, and then hear a lecture how I wasn't giving it my all like Kelli. Teachers at school would even compare me to her.

I couldn't understand why Kelli never wanted me to touch her belongings. She touched mine all the time and that was okay, but yet I wasn't allowed to even sit on her bed without being yelled at.

Was this behavior I just learned a way to be more like the other girls? I wanted to fit in with the other kids my age. I felt awkward and different. Maybe it could be the answer to my problems.

I could hear giggling in the hallway and looked up to see what was going on. All three girls were standing over me trying to see if I was asleep.

"You asleep, Courteney?" they asked giggling.

"Sorry to disappoint you, but no. You can't do the prank on me tonight. I'm not first asleep," I said smiling.

We all started laughing and curled up into our sleeping bags to settle in for the night. All four of us gazed out the window at the moonlit sky and talked about what boys we thought were cute until the early hours of the morning.

Olivia, Tatum, and Susie finally fell into a peaceful sleep. I couldn't believe I was the last asleep. I grabbed their bras and headed for the kitchen. It was payback time.

I lay back down after finishing my business in the kitchen and looked at my three friends. How I wished that the girls in my class could be as nice as these girls.

I could feel the unshed tears starting to burn my eyes. I put my head down into my pillow and started to cry softly fearing I would wake the others.

What is wrong with me? Why can't I be like the other girls? I knew what I had to do to be more like them. I would do it, I had to. It was frightening, and I knew I could never tell anyone. This was my secret.

My Decision

Another Monday was approaching, which meant I had to go back to school and deal with Sami Jo and the gang. It had been a fun weekend with the Friday night slumber party and shopping on Saturday with my mother and sister.

Kelli had taken one of her friends, Pam, shopping with us. They went off by themselves, so that left mom and I enjoying the day together. We had an enjoyable taco lunch at the Mexican food restaurant in the mall. She bought me the cutest outfit from Dillard's. Mom and I loved shopping together, and she was always kind about buying all of us new clothes.

Today had been one of those fun-filled Sundays with dad. Mom did her usual and played the piano at church. She was a wonderful musician and I did enjoy listening to her play. We were always given a choice of going to church with mom or going out to play with dad. Most of the times I choose to go with dad. I didn't see much use in my life for church and I had a hard time staying awake anyway. The things we got to do with dad were more exciting.

Our adventure today was bowling, hiking, and riding bikes. Kelli had plans with friends, but John and I got in on all the fun. John just loves to bowl because he usually beats everyone. Of course, sometimes we let him win because he's the youngest and it makes him feel good. I figure mom and dad probably let me win games too when I was younger.

Now it was Sunday evening, and I was dreading another week of school.

"Courteney, have you showered and brushed your teeth yet?" asked mom standing in my bedroom doorway.

"No, but I'll do it now," I said knowing it was getting late.

"Is everything okay at school, Courteney? Those girls aren't giving you a hard time are they?" Mom asked with concern.

"Everything is fine. I need to get ready for bed now," I said wanting to avoid the subject.

I went into the bathroom to get ready for bed and stopped in front of the toilet. Ever since the slumber party on Friday night I have been thinking about what happened. Every time I looked at a toilet now it reminded me of this new behavior that scared me. I wasn't ready to try it yet, but I knew I would. I didn't want anyone in my family to hear what I was doing. I knew I should probably do it when they were out of the house.

"What are you doing?" asked Kelli startling me.

"I'm just getting ready for bed. I need to get a shower, but I'll hurry so you can get ready for bed too," I told Kelli.

"That's okay. Dylan is supposed to call and I'll be talking with him for a while," Kelli said walking out of the bathroom.

Dylan was Kelli's boyfriend. He was a nice guy and really cute too. He was tall and had dark brown hair. I enjoy when he comes over to the house for dinner, because Kelli is always nicer to me when he is around.

I took a quick shower, brushed my teeth, and told everyone goodnight. I was tired from the weekend and was feeling kind of down. I disliked Sunday nights. I knew the next day would bring five days of dealing with those girls. I truly dreaded that thought.

I lay down in the warmth of my bed and pulled the quilt up around me. My grandmother had made this quilt for me when I was a little girl. It had white blocks with little girls in each block that wore different colored dresses. The backing was a yellowish color. It was beautiful, and I enjoyed curling up in this handmade quilt at night.

I hadn't seen my grandparents in quite sometime now, because my parents were always upset with them. Their solution to their disagreements was to walk away from them. It was a sad thought to think I would not speak with or see them again for quite sometime. At least I had my quilt that reminded me of them and our good times together.

I hoped that no one would come into my room to check on me. I wanted to be alone to sort through my feelings.

Sometimes I feel so angry inside that I could just start screaming at people, but I knew that I would say things that would be hurtful. If someone took the time to get to know me, they would discover that I didn't want to hurt anyone's feelings. Even when somebody was terrible to me, I just didn't have the heart to hurt them back.

Dad tells me to just forget about what those girls say and to get on with life and be happy, but I can't. He makes it sound so simple, but it's easier said than done. I'm not sure why I just can't let it go, but I can't. This bothers me and makes me feel like I am different than everyone else. I closed my eyes. I could feel tears starting to burn my eyes, and threatening to fall.

My head started throbbing. I knew I needed to relax so I didn't end up with a migraine. I had taken migraine medicine before bed so hopefully it would prevent me from getting one tonight. I wiped away the tears that started to trickle down my cheek.

I leaned over and hit the power button on my stereo that sits on my night stand. I loved to listen to my cassette tape of Kenny Rogers when I went to bed. I lay there listening to the soft music and started to feel relaxed. My favorite song, "Lady," was playing. I dreamed of someday getting to see Kenny Rogers perform live and finally found sleep dreaming of this dream.

The next day at school wasn't going to bad until lunch time. I got into the lunch line and sure enough, Sami Jo and the gang hopped into line right behind me. I could hear pig sounds and giggling. Anger started to boil inside of me, but I knew I couldn't say anything to them.

"We've been looking for you today, Courteney. Have you been avoiding us?" Shelly said with sarcasm in her voice.

Shelly was tall, had extremely short blonde hair, and a nose that seemed to go on forever. The only reason she was popular was because she was Sami Jo's live puppet. She stayed popular as long as she did exactly what Sami Jo told her to do.

I kept reminding myself to be nice, it isn't nice to be mean. Don't be like them.

"No, I've been around," I responded.

I picked up my lunch tray and headed to go sit by Kirsten, but noticed that all the seats around her were already taken. I searched for the closest open seat and quickly sat down before they could say anything else. I just wanted to eat and get out of there.

Cindy walked up with a smirk on her face and said, "You think you really need to eat all of that food, Courteney? It'll just make you fatter and uglier than you already are."

I could hear all four of them laughing and snorting behind me. I could feel the tears starting to burn my eyes and wished I wasn't such a sensitive person.

"Can you demonstrate for us how a pig eats?" Cindy said laughing.

I could feel the eyes of many others on me wondering what I would say or do. Everyone knew me well enough to know I wasn't going to do anything. I just wasn't the kind of person to fight back and had been taught not to be mean to others.

I couldn't fight back the tears any longer. Tears starting streaming down my face and I could feel my body temperature rising. I felt hot and faint. I jumped up from the cafeteria table and ran out of the lunch room. I didn't even bother to put my tray up, nor had I eaten a bite. I ran to the nearest restroom and started getting sick to my stomach. My entire body shook and the room was spinning so fast that I collapsed to the ground in tears.

"Courteney, are you okay?" Mrs. Ulrich asked with concern. I hadn't even realized that a teacher had walked into the restroom.

"I'm sick. Can you please get someone to take me home?" I asked sobbing.

"Let's get you to the office to lie down, and we'll call your dad to take you home." Mrs. Ulrich was such a nice teacher. I knew her concern was sincere.

"Thanks. Let mom know that I am going home, would you?"

"Sure."

Dad was there in no time to take me home. I just told him my stomach hurt and I was dizzy. That was the truth, but I didn't tell him what happened at lunch. I knew he wouldn't understand.

"Will you be okay at the house by yourself, Courteney?" he asked with concern.

"Yes, Dad, I'll be fine. I'm just going to lie down and get some sleep. Thanks for the ride."

I walked into the house and went into the bathroom to wash my face with a cool rag. My entire body was trembling, and I felt like I was burning up. I was wiping my forehead with the cool rag when I caught sight of the toilet through the bathroom mirror. I just stood there not knowing what to do, and then I did it.

I went into the kitchen and started eating everything I knew was sinful and full of calories. I ate ice cream, cookies, cake, donuts, and everything I could find that was junk food. I didn't just eat little bits of each. I ate huge amounts that I'm sure added up to thousands of calories. I was definitely out of control, but for a short period of time it gave me this weird feeling of power and control.

That feeling of power didn't last long though. I had eaten so much I was feeling sick to my stomach and very guilty about how much I had eaten. I ran to the bathroom and started to make myself vomit. It was an awful feeling and my body shook each time food came back up, but I knew I had to do it. I had to get all of the food out of me.

After I just couldn't get sick anymore, I flushed the toilet and washed my hands and face. I felt so tired suddenly. I wanted to sleep, but first I had to get rid of the evidence in the kitchen. I threw all the wrappers away and rearranged items in the kitchen cabinets hoping that mom wouldn't notice that a lot of the junk food was missing. I didn't think she would notice. The kitchen looked put back in proper order as far as I could tell.

I felt so weak. It was like all of the energy had been drained from my body. I needed to lie down and get some sleep. I crawled underneath the soft, warm blankets of my bed and quickly fell into a deep sleep.

"Courteney... Courteney, are you feeling better?" asked mom shaking my shoulder lightly.

I was sleeping so soundly that I hadn't even heard anyone come home.

"I'm feeling a little better mom, but I'm still tired. I just want to sleep."

"Okay, but holler if you need anything," Mom said with concern.

"I will, Mom," I said turning over and pulling the covers closer to me.

Mom left the room, but I couldn't fall back to sleep right away. I laid there and thought about everything that happened today.

The anger I felt inside towards those girls was more than I could handle. I couldn't figure out how to make things better and being nice sure wasn't working. But I couldn't be mean, that wasn't right either. I wished I had somebody to talk to. Maybe somebody else would have an idea of how to make things better.

I leaned over and turned on my stereo. I could hear the soothing voice of Kenny Rogers singing. I closed my eyes and started to relax.

I could hear John knocking softly at the door, "Courteney... Courteney."

"Come on in, John."

"Mom says dinner is ready. Do you want to eat?"

"Tell mom I'm not hungry."

"I love you, Courteney. Do you love me?" asked John.

"Yes, I love you, John. I'm just not feeling well tonight. Goodnight."

John shut the door and I could hear him running to tell mom I didn't want any dinner. I figured mom would come and inquire why I didn't want to eat, but she didn't.

Surprisingly, I did feel hungry. After all the food I ate you would think I'd be full for the next week. I hoped that when I made myself get sick I got all of that food out of my system, but I just wasn't sure. What if I didn't? How much weight would I gain from eating that large amount of food? I will just eat very little for the next day or two so it'll make up for all the calories

I consumed. I felt so guilty and ashamed inside about eating so much food. What if somebody found out? I'll just be careful, no one will find out.

I stared at the ceiling and listened to music. I just knew that my decision to try this new behavior would help me lose weight and solve my problems.

The next few days at school were about the same as always. I tried to dodge Sami Jo and the gang, and they usually found me. My stomach was cramping and talking to me because I had hardly eaten anything in three days to make up for consuming tons of calories the other day. I felt shaky, but somehow I managed.

I looked forward to the end of each school day because of dance practice. We were getting ready for a performance tomorrow, Friday, and I was excited about the routine we were doing. It was a dance to the song, "I Feel for You" by Chaka Chan. We had learned this routine at camp this summer and hadn't performed it in front of the school yet. It was a great routine and the entire team was excited about performing at the school assembly.

I had also decided to start exercising more. My dad was a jogger, so I started taking an interest in jogging. The first day I went for a run, I ran one mile. I didn't think that was too bad considering I had never done this before. My stomach was cramping a lot while I was jogging, but I kept on going until I accomplished my goal of a mile.

I could hear my sister talking on the phone in her room to her boyfriend. She spent a lot of time talking on the phone with him. I didn't blame her though. If I had a boyfriend, I guess I'd like to talk on the phone with him.

I was hanging out in my room by myself listening to music and reading a book. It felt good to relax after a long day at school, dance practice, and jogging my mile.

"Courteney," Kelli said coming into my room without knocking.

"What, Kelli?"

"You were in my closet. What did you take?" she asked harshly.

"I wasn't in your closet, Kelli. I didn't take any of your clothes," I responded.

Kelli caught me off guard with a slap across my face. My left cheek stung and I could feel the tears threatening to come.

"You're lying, Courteney. I know you are. No wonder no one likes you, you're ugly and you stink. If you even tell mom and dad that I slapped you, you will be in trouble. Do you understand?" Kelli said storming out of my room.

It all happened so fast I didn't even have time to respond before Kelli slammed my door. I threw myself onto my bed and cried myself to sleep.

I was furious at my sister for what she had said to me last night. I didn't say anything to mom or dad, but I did give my sister the cold shoulder. I was determined to not let her ruin my day. It was Friday and we were performing our dance routine at the school assembly. We wore our green and white pleated skirts with our green vest that had AJHS on them. All of us had our hair pulled back in pony tails with green and white ribbons tied in bows.

Sami Jo, Shelly, Cindy, and Tami were surprisingly being nice to me today. I didn't understand why, but I'd accept the kindness anytime they were willing to give it.

I was grabbing my books out of my locker for Science when all four walked up to my locker.

Cautiously, I said, "Hi."

"Hi, Courteney," all four responded cheerfully.

"I hear the dance team is performing at the pep assembly today," said Cindy.

"Yes, we are. We're performing a dance we learned at camp this summer," I replied.

"I bet you'll do a great job. You always do," said Sami Jo.

"We were wondering if you'd like to come to a party tomorrow night at Lori's house. It's just a small get together. It starts around seven o'clock. Would you like to come?" asked Shelly.

"Sure, that would be great," I said excitedly.

"Great, see you there. Good luck at the assembly," all four said smiling.

I shut my locker and turned to go to class. I couldn't believe they had invited me to one of their parties. Lori was one of Sami Jo's followers. Sometimes she was nice to me, and sometimes she wasn't. She went along with whatever Sami Jo and her gang were doing. A lot of the parties took place at her house. I hoped that mom and dad would let me go. This was great. Maybe they were going to start being nice to me now.

The school assembly went great. Everyone on the dance team performed the routine perfectly and the kids at school seemed to love it. Even Sami Jo and the gang came up to all of us as we were leaving school and told us how great we performed.

"Don't forget about the party tomorrow night at seven," said Sami Jo.

"I won't, see you then," I responded excitedly.

I wasn't sure how to approach mom about the Saturday night party at Lori's house. I knew if mom approved of me going, it would be fine with dad. So I figured I better just ask her. We were in the car going home from school when I finally got my nerve up to ask.

"Mom, I was invited to a party at Lori's house tomorrow night. Do you think I could go?" I asked nervously.

"Who is going to be there?" asked mom.

"I think it's just going to be Lori, Sami Jo, Shelly, Cindy, and Tami. I'm not sure who else was invited," I said honestly.

"What about parents? Are there going to be adults there?" asked my protective mother.

"I'm sure Lori's parents will be there, they usually are."

"I'm not sure about this, Courteney. Those girls aren't always nice to you. They've invited you places before and set you up. Remember when they invited you to the movies and they never showed. Why are they all of a sudden being nice?"

"Please, Mom. I really want to go. They were really nice to me today. They'll be nice to me at the party. Please," I said pleadingly.

"Well, if you really want to go I'll let you."

We were home now and I cheerfully got out of the car and gave mom a warm hug and told her, "Thanks. Everything will be fine, Mom; you'll see."

I just knew this was going to be a great weekend.

The Party

Saturday had included the usual routine of household chores and lawn work. Unfortunately, my chores were all inside the house. I would've enjoyed doing chores outside on this beautiful autumn day.

The trees were starting to turn multi-colored with their shades of red, orange, and yellow showing. The heat of the summer was finally disappearing with the days beginning to feel cool and crisp. I was trying to hurry through my chores, which included cleaning my bedroom and bathroom, so I could go outside for my daily jog and enjoy this magnificent day.

"Courteney. John. Kelli. Time for lunch."

I could hear Mom's call coming from the kitchen along with the wonderful aroma of lasagna and homemade bread. This was one of my favorite meals, but I wasn't sure if I should eat. I was hungry because of not eating breakfast, but I didn't want to gain weight. I had actually lost a few pounds and didn't want to gain it back. Maybe it wouldn't hurt just to eat a little. I was hungry, and I didn't want to be starving going to the party tonight.

Kelli and John were already eating by the time I walked into the kitchen.

"It smells great, Mom," I said grabbing a plate.

"Thanks. What time does the party start tonight, Courteney?" Mom asked.

"Seven o'clock. I was thinking Kelli could just give me a ride when she goes over to Dylan's house for dinner," I replied.

"That would be fine, but I want you to promise that if those girls start being mean to you that you will call me so I can come and get you," said Mom.

"That's fine, Mom; I promise. The lasagna is great," I said trying to get off the topic of the party.

I was definitely excited about this party, but I knew mom didn't think it was a great idea for me to go.

"Would you like another piece of lasagna, Courteney?" Mom asked dishing another piece out of the hot pan.

"No thanks, Mom. One piece is plenty."

I could've eaten another piece, but I knew I didn't need it. My stomach was still growling, but it would just have to be satisfied.

I placed my plate in the sink and went to finish my chores. I wanted to exercise and get a shower before I headed to Lori's house for the party. I was planning on wearing my new outfit mom had purchased for me last weekend when we went shopping. The jeans were khaki colored with dainty blue and yellow flowers on the front and back pockets. It had a light weight, v-neck, blue sweater trimmed in flowers to match the pants. Blue is my favorite color to wear, because it accents my baby blue eyes.

I had already cleaned the bathroom and dusted my room, but I needed to pick up my room before I could call it quits. The biggest drawback to chores was having mom inspect our work. She had to give the okay before we knew we were finished.

Quickly, I put everything in its place and wandered back into the kitchen to let mom know I was finished and ready for inspection. It was pretty easy to pass one of her inspections, but I always worried I would have to redo the bathroom. I hated cleaning the bathroom, but it was my week to clean it. I knew I had to if I wanted to go to the party.

"Great, I'll check your chores if you'll help finish the dishes," said Mom.

"Sure, that's fine, Mom," I replied.

Dishes weren't a problem. I enjoyed cooking and cleaning dishes.

"Courteney. Courteney. Come look what I found," John shouted excitedly from the front door.

"What is it?" I asked John.

"Look, I found a turtle."

"Wow, that's neat John. Are you going to keep it and give it a name?" I asked knowing mom probably wouldn't let him.

"No, I'm going to take it down to the pond at the country club and let it go. Tell mom I'll be back shortly," he said running off down the hill.

"Where's John going?" Mom asked startling me.

"Oh, he found a turtle and he's taking it down to the pond at the country club. He told me to tell you he won't be long. Did my bedroom and bathroom look okay?" I asked hoping it was.

"Yes, everything was fine."

"Thanks, Mom. Dishes are finished and I wiped off the table. I'm going out for a run. Be back after a while."

After running and a shower, I retreated quickly to my bedroom to get ready for the party. Hurriedly, I dressed in my new outfit and went to fix my hair. It seemed like it took forever to do my hair and makeup.

My hair has a lot of body and wave and has its own mind at times. I wanted to wear it down, but it just wasn't turning out how I wanted it to. I didn't want to put it in a ponytail. That is how I wore it most days to school, especially with dance practice every-day. Finally, I settled for pulling part of it up, pinned it with a bar-rette, and let the rest hang down in the back.

I stepped back from the vanity and looked at myself in the mir-ror. Even though I had been exercising and lost a few pounds, I still looked heavy. My face has this pudgy, baby face look that I just don't find attractive. All the other girls in my class seemed to be getting their womanly figures, but I just didn't seem to be filling out in the right places. My mother says it's just baby fat and I'll lose it, but I'm beginning to wonder. I stared at myself in the mirror and wished I could feel better about how I looked. I wanted to look and feel pretty for this party. I wanted these girls to like me.

Knowing I needed to hurry and eat dinner before I left, I decided there was nothing more I could do to improve my look for the evening. I headed for the kitchen to prepare something to eat when I heard the front doorbell ring.

"Who could that be?" I muttered to myself.

"I'll get it. I'll get it," John hollered running down the hallway to the front door.

John opened the door with a cheerful, "Hello."

"Hi. Is Courteney here?" asked Sami Jo.

It was still about two hours before the party was supposed to start. What was Sami Jo doing here? I took a deep breath, unconsciously straightened my shoulders to appear confident, and walked up to the door. I could feel the muscles in my stomach tighten and my entire body started to tremble. The last thing I wanted was for Sami Jo to think I was nervous. I had to get control of myself.

Touching John on the shoulder I said, "Thanks, John. I got it."

He took off out the front door and ran across the street to play with a neighbor boy.

"Hi," I said smiling nervously at Sami Jo.

"I thought you might want a ride to the party. Are you ready to go?" asked Sami Jo cheerfully.

"Well, I do need to eat dinner first. I could be ready in about twenty minutes if that is okay," I replied.

"Lori was planning on having some food there for us to eat. You can just eat with us if you would like."

"Sure, that would be great. I need to ask my mother first," I said knowing I'd be in trouble if I didn't. I opened the door wide gesturing for Sami Jo to come indoors. "Come on in while I ask. Feel free to sit down while I find my mother," I said pointing to the couch in the front room.

Knowing mom was downstairs in the basement, I quickly ran down the stairs to get permission.

Out of breath, I asked, "Mom, Sami Jo is here and wants to give me a ride to the party. Is that okay?"

Mom sighed deeply. "Are you sure about going to this party, Courteney? You know these girls aren't always nice to you. I hate to see your feelings get hurt again by them," she stated.

"Please, Mom, I'll be fine. I'll call if things aren't going well. I promise."

She wrapped her arms around me and gave me one of her welcomed warm hugs.

"Okay, Courteney, but please be careful. Be home no later than ten thirty to eleven o'clock. I love you," she said giving me a kiss on the forehead.

"Thanks, Mom. I love you too," I said giving her a kiss on the cheek.

I sprinted back up the stairs, grabbed my denim jacket, and headed out the door with Sami Jo. Surely, this was going to be a great evening.

The ride to Lori's house was a quick five minute drive. She didn't live but a couple miles from my house. I was extremely nervous, but I couldn't tell if Sami Jo noticed or not. She didn't say much to me, but she did compliment my outfit. I thanked her for the compliment and started to tell her where I had purchased it, but she didn't seem too interested. I was glad when we pulled into Lori's driveway so I wouldn't have to think of something else to say.

When we walked into Lori's house you could smell wonderful aromas coming from the kitchen. Lori's mom, Mrs. White, was busily preparing supper for all of us. Mrs. White was always nice to me when I saw her around town. She always made a point to stop and say hello. Sami Jo didn't stop to speak with her, but I thought it would be polite to at least say hello.

"Hi, Mrs. White," I said with a smile.

"Hi, Courteney. How are you? How are your parents?" she asked.

"We're all fine. Is there anything I can help you with in the kitchen?"

"No thanks, you enjoy yourself and join the other girls in the family room. I think they are playing darts and pool. I'll have supper ready in a few minutes," she said taking a hot casserole dish out of the oven.

I would've rather stayed in the kitchen to help Mrs. White

prepare supper, but I knew I had to join the other girls and hope for the best. My stomach felt like it was tied into so many knots that I didn't know if I'd be able to speak and get the words out correctly.

I reluctantly headed down the hallway and into the family room where Sami Jo, Shelly, Cindy, Tami, and Lori were all playing games and listening to music.

"Hi, Courteney," they all said simultaneously.

"Come play darts with us," Cindy said cheerfully.

"I'm not sure how to play. I've never played before," I said feeling a little dim-witted.

"Don't worry, we'll teach you," responded Tami cheerfully.

Things were going pretty good. Cindy and Tami taught me to play darts and were very helpful in teaching me how to keep score. We played a couple of games until it was suppertime.

Supper was delicious. Mrs. White was a magnificent cook. She baked a chicken casserole dish, bread sticks, and a wonderful Caesar salad.

"The food is wonderful, Mrs. White. You'll have to give this recipe to my mother," I said hoping she wouldn't fail to remember.

"Sure, Courteney. I'm pleased you like it," Mrs. White said smiling.

The other girls didn't say much through supper. When they finished they immediately went back to the family room to play games and listen to music.

"Would you like help with the dishes, Mrs. White?" I asked while helping her clear the table off.

"Oh thanks, Courteney, but you go ahead and play with the girls. I'm just going to put the dishes in the dishwasher, and then my husband and I are going to the seven o'clock movie at the theatre downtown."

"Oh, I didn't know you were going anywhere. That sounds like fun," I said feeling my heart drop.

So far the girls were being nice, but what would it be like when the adults were absent. They had a tendency to change for the worse when there weren't adults around. I finally convinced myself to just relax and enjoy myself and went back into the family room to join the other girls.

An hour had passed, Mr. and Mrs. White had gone to the movies, and the girls were still being pleasant. I had begun to relax around them and was enjoying the evening. I was getting ready to start a game of pool against Sami Jo when I heard the front door bell ring.

Lori hurriedly ran to the door to greet five guys that I didn't recognize. I wondered if her mother and father knew about these guys coming to the party. They appeared to be older than all of us, and I definitely knew they weren't in our class. It made me a bit nervous having them here, because I knew my parents wouldn't approve without adult supervision. I wasn't about to say anything for fear that they would laugh at my worries.

All of them headed to the screened in porch on the backside of the house. All of the other girls seemed to know them, but they never did introduce me to these guys. I walked out onto the porch where they were listening to music and talking. The evening had turned out to be a cool autumn night with a full moon, and hundreds of shining stars. It truly was a beautiful night. I didn't know what to say, so I just stood there.

"Hey, Courteney, would you mind helping me get drinks for everyone?" asked Lori standing up and walking over to me.

"Sure," I said following her into the kitchen.

We filled eleven glasses full of ice and put an assortment of soda pop on a tray.

"Lori. Did your parents know these guys were coming over? I don't want you to get into trouble," I asked reluctantly not wanting to spoil the party.

"No, but they're not staying long. They'll be gone before my parents get back from the movie," she said picking up the tray of sodas.

I picked up the tray of glasses and followed her to the back porch where everyone was still sitting and talking.

"Courteney, would you mind doing us a favor?" Sami Jo asked

giving me one of her charming smiles. "We want to take some pictures and the guys have a camera in their van. It's in the back pocket of the driver's seat. Would you mind getting it for us? The sliding door is unlocked on the van."

"Yea, I'll get it," I responded.

I grabbed my denim jacket, knowing it was chilly outside, and headed out the front door. Their van was sitting in the driveway so I didn't have far to walk. I grabbed the handle on the sliding door and slid the door open. I crawled in on my hands and knees and reached into the pocket, but I couldn't feel a camera.

Suddenly, I heard the driver's door open and one of the guys get into the van. I could hear footsteps and giggling coming from behind me. I turned around to see Sami Jo, Shelly, Cindy, Tami, Lori, and the other four guys standing at the opening of the sliding door. The four guys hopped into the van and blocked me from getting out. Terror started to overtake me, and I could feel myself shaking. I knew something horrible was about to happen. I could feel it.

"The guys are going to take you for a ride, Courteney. You have a good time and don't do anything we wouldn't do," Sami Jo said, laughing along with the other girls.

I tried to push my way past the two guys nearest the door, but they stopped me and pushed me back behind the driver's seat.

"These guys are fun to be with, Courteney. You'll have a great time," Shelly said laughing.

I pulled my legs up as close to my chest as I could get them and put my head down on my knees. I heard the sliding door shut, and could feel the van pulling out of the driveway.

The tears were rolling down my cheeks, because I knew what these girls had planned for me. I had never been with a guy before, and I didn't want my first experience to be with five guys forcing themselves on me. My entire body shook with uncontrollable sobs and the fear I felt was astonishing.

They had tricked me into coming to this party, and once again I had been set up. This was by far the worst trick they had played on me. What was I going to do? What would happen to me? I have heard of things like this on the news before. Some girls wind up disappearing, or are found in a river months later. Would I ever see my family again? My mind was racing with horrible thoughts, and I knew I needed to take control of my fear.

I didn't know what direction the van was headed and thought it would be to my advantage if I knew where they were taking me. Maybe if I knew where they were going, I could jump out of the van and run away from them and hide. Trying to control my sobs, I slowly pulled myself up into the seat behind the driver's seat.

"Stay on the floor," one of the guys hollered at me.

Immediately, I sunk back down on the floor and curled my legs up to my chest. My sobs, once again, were uncontrollable, and I felt totally helpless against these five big guys.

"What is your name?" one guy asked me.

Sobbing I said, "Courteney… Courteney Baker."

"Are you related to Mrs. Baker, the teacher at the junior high?"

"Yes, I'm her daughter," I replied trying to control myself.

I didn't know any of their names. They were careful not to say them in front of me. One of them, he had dark hair and was the biggest of the guys, apparently knew my mother. He started talking with the rest of them.

"I know this girl's mother. I don't think it's a good idea to do this. I like her mom and if anyone ever found out, we'd be in big trouble."

"Stop being a wimp," one of the other guys retorted.

"It's not about being a wimp. If we do what those girls want us to do, we can end up in prison. Do you want to go to prison?" he hollered back at the other guy. "I know where she lives. Let's just drop her off on the back roads near her house."

One of them asked me, "Courteney, if we don't hurt you, do you promise not to tell anyone about this?"

"I promise," I responded so quickly I didn't even have time to think about my answer. I just wanted out of this van. "You can drop me off on the back roads, I'll walk home. I promise not to say a word."

I sat there on the floor shaking, and hoping that they were really going to take me somewhere and drop me off. The big guy with dark hair told the driver where to go. We drove past my house, and then turned left on the dirt road down the street. He drove about a mile out on the dirt road, and then suddenly the van came to a stop.

My heart felt like it had stopped. I didn't think I was going to be able to move. How I hoped they would keep their word.

The guy closest to the sliding door slid it open and told me to get out. I looked at all of them for a few seconds not knowing if they were serious or tricking me. I finally got up my nerve to slide across the carpeted floor and slid out of the van.

One of the guys grabbed my arm forcefully and stated firmly, "You promised not to say anything. Don't forget, because if you do we will find you. We will carry out what those girls wanted us to do. Understand?"

"Yes, I understand. I won't forget," I replied trying to stop crying.

The door shut on the van and they skidded off down the road. Dirt and rocks were being flung into the darkness of the night. I covered my face to prevent from being hit by one of the rocks.

I stood in the middle of the road for a few minutes dumbfounded by what had just taken place. I looked up at the night sky and was thankful for a bright, full moon. At least I would have a little light to guide me on my journey home. I knew this road well. I had ridden four wheelers back here before. I wasn't too far from home. It was chilly, so I started walking at a fast pace to try and keep warm.

I felt relieved that those guys decided not to hurt me, but what if they changed their minds and came back for me. I started getting myself all worked up and scared of what could still happen. Tears started running down my cold cheeks, and I picked up my pace to a slow jog. It took about ten minutes to reach our neighborhood. As soon as I felt safe, I slowed my pace to a brisk walk.

What was I going to tell my mother? She would probably be up reading a book and waiting for me to get home. She'd want a full report on the evening. Somehow I would have to avoid her.

Suzi started barking and ran up to greet me.

I bent down to pick her up saying, "Hi, girl."

Suddenly, an idea came to me. "Okay, girl, you have to help me out. You want to go inside with me?" I said hugging her and kissing her forehead. She must've liked the idea because I received one of her wet, sloppy kisses.

I quietly opened the backdoor and could see the light on in the front room. I knew mom was lying on the couch reading, even though a fireplace was blocking my view of her.

"Hey, Mom, I'm home. I'm taking Suzi downstairs with me to listen to the jukebox."

"Did you have a nice time? Were the girls nice to you?" she asked still lying on the couch.

"Yes, everything was fine. I'll see you in the morning," I replied wanting to avoid further conversation.

I quickly headed down the stairs and turned on the jukebox. The strobe lights lit the room and the song, "Annie's Song" by John Denver was playing. I lay down on the couch with Suzi and pulled a blanket over us. It felt so good to be safe at home with my dog in my arms.

My thoughts turned to Sami Jo and the other girls. How could they plan such a terrible scheme against me? I could feel the anger starting to boil inside of me. I was more than upset with these girls. I was infuriated with them, but yet scared to death what they would try next. What if I didn't get so lucky next time? I pulled Suzi closer to me and the tears started falling uncontrollably.

I could hear the laughter of the girls and them saying, "Don't do anything I wouldn't do. You'll have fun."

Should I tell someone about what happened? No, I promised those guys I wouldn't. What if I break my promise? Would they come after me? I wasn't taking any chances. I would just have to bury my anger and act like nothing had happened. I wanted to share my fears and anger with someone, but I knew this would have to be my secret.

Secrets

I could hear everyone already moving around upstairs when I woke up. My body felt achy and tired from tossing and turning all night. I knew I had to face the day ahead of me but didn't really feel like being around everyone. I made myself get up, even though my entire body just wanted to curl up under the warm covers and not function all day.

Suzi came running to me, letting me know she wanted to go outside.

"Hi, girl. I almost forgot you slept with me last night. We need to get you outside," I said knowing mom wouldn't be pleased to find her in the house. I took her upstairs and let her out the back door before anyone knew she had been in the house all night.

Dad came around the corner ready for the day. "Hi, Courteney. Are you coming with me today? Your mom has already left for church."

"No thanks, Dad. I think I'll stay home today and work on schoolwork."

"Are you sure? Kelli and John are coming with me. You'll be by yourself," Dad stated sincerely.

"That's okay. I have to get some things finished for school. See you later," I replied quietly slipping into my room and shutting the door.

The quiet day by myself didn't end up being a pleasant one. I kept thinking about the party, those guys, the ride in the van, and what those girls had planned. I knew I had to go to school tomorrow and face Sami Jo and the gang. What would I say to them?

How would they treat me? I ended up back in the kitchen eating thousands of calories as quickly as I could, then the feelings of guilt and shame soon followed. After I finished vomiting as much food as I could get back up, I lay in my bed and cried. My body felt so tired, and I soon cried myself to sleep.

School the next day wasn't pleasant. It actually turned out to be a very short day. I had this gut feeling that something was going to happen, but not quite sure what that something was going to be.

The first couple hours of school were good enough, but after second hour English, I needed to go to my locker and get some books for my next class. I opened my locker and saw there was something inside. It was several sheets of paper folded over and stapled together to make a book. It had my name on the front, so I knew it was intended for me. By glancing at the carefully drawn, descriptive, offensive pictures, and appalling words; I knew this was not a kind note. I knew immediately who it was from. Tears started burning my eyes.

"What's the matter, Courteney? Don't you think our drawings are good?" asked Sami Jo sarcastically.

I jerked around to find Sami Jo and many of her followers standing around me. I thought I was going to be sick to my stomach and humiliate myself even more than I already was. Even though I knew it wasn't a good idea to cry, I couldn't stop the tears from flowing. I wanted to run out of the school and never turn back. There were so many people standing around me, that I couldn't go anywhere. I wasn't the kind of person to fight back, so if everyone was expecting a fight, they were going to be highly disappointed.

"What's the matter, Courteney? Didn't you have fun Saturday night?" Shelly asked shoving me against the lockers. I could feel the pain shoot through my head when it slammed against the metal lockers.

"What's going on? Break it up," said one of the teachers working her way through the crowd.

When the teacher made it through the group of students, she stood staring at me. I can only imagine how she must've felt finding her daughter in the center of the heated crowd of kids. I stood there for a few seconds staring at my mother, also a teacher trying to do her job, and crying as I held this dreadful note in my quivering hands. I had enough and couldn't do this anymore.

I took off running to the counselors' office. Why I ran there I'm not sure. The school counselor, Mr. Payne, was a very nice person. I had talked with him several times before about these girls. I just didn't know where else to go.

Running into his office unannounced and sobbing I yelled, "I want to go home. I don't ever want to come back to this school again."

Startled by someone bursting through his door, he jumped to his feet. "Calm down, Courteney. What happened? Here, Courteney," sliding a chair up behind me, "sit down and let me get you something cool to drink."

My mother came walking into his office trying to keep herself in complete control of the situation, but yet I could tell she was fuming on the inside. Her hands were shaking and tears were flowing freely down her cheeks.

"Let me see the note they gave you, Courteney," she demanded sternly.

I hadn't read everything in it, but I knew by the descriptive pictures and the few words I had read that it wasn't kind. Still crying, I reluctantly handed it to my mother. I could see her glancing at the pages in the paper book and handing it to Mr. Payne.

"I want to go home, Mom," I demanded with uncontrollable sobs shaking my entire body.

"I'll call your father," she responded picking up the phone in Mr. Payne's office.

That was my last day at Atchison Junior High School. I knew I would miss being on the dance team and rooming with Kirsten at summer camps. Music and dancing were my passion, but the fear I felt outweighed my passion for the dance team. What would those girls plan for me next? Is running away from the problem the correct thing to do? I wasn't sure what the answer to these questions should be, but I knew this, I never wanted to face Sami

Jo and her gang again. The pain they inflicted on me was obviously more than I could handle.

By Friday, my parents had decided that they would send me to a different school. I had stayed home all week waiting for my parents to decide which school I should attend. They were looking at three different schools as possibilities. There was a Catholic school in town, a Lutheran school in Leavenworth, and a small country school in Effingham that they were considering. I'm not sure what qualities in a school they were looking for, but the end result was I was to attend Atchison County Community High School in Effingham, Kansas.

Effingham was a small, rural community about thirty minutes west of Atchison. Dad and I drove out there over the weekend to check out the town and my new school. It was a small community with downtown consisting of two blocks. There weren't fast food restaurants or movie theatres where the teenagers could hangout. Amazingly, there was a public pool, a small grocery store, and two pubs as the main attractions. Not much for teenagers to do, but it was a pleasant little town. Anyhow, I would only be going to school there, not living here.

I was excited about the fact that I would be in high school now and not junior high. My parents had informed me that there wasn't a dance team at this school, but the school was known for its magnificent, sizeable band. There were about a hundred and seventy-five students in the school with over a hundred of them in the band. My mother knew the band director, Mr. Linn, and knew he was an exceptional director. This was exciting news since I played the clarinet and was a twirler.

"So what do you think of Effingham? Do you think you'll like going to school there, Courteney?" Dad asked on the drive home.

"It seems nice, Dad. I'm certain I'll like it better than having to deal with Sami Jo and her gang," I replied.

"Courteney, you can't let people bring you down. Don't let those girls get the best of you," he stated.

"I know, Dad. I really don't want to talk about those girls anymore," I replied with tears filling my eyes.

Patting my knee, Dad stated, "I love you, Courteney. Everything is going to get better."

Shortly after we arrived back home, I set out for my daily jog. It was a great way to have alone time, and reflect on all the good and bad that life brought my way.

It would be tough starting all over in high school and having to make new friends. I wanted to leave the bad experiences behind me and have a fresh start at a new school. I was thankful that I was getting the opportunity to go to a different school, and could feel it was going to be a positive change in my life.

Atchison County Community High School
1982–1985

I'd have to say that my high school years were good, but not wonderful. There were the normal cliques that each student belonged to, but thankfully, none were as mean and vindictive as Sami Jo and her gang. My overall experience was educational, and I enjoyed playing in the large band, being a baton twirler, and being a wrestling cheerleader. From an outsiders view I appeared to be a typical happy, energetic teenager.

There was a secretive side of me that many didn't know, and my biggest downfall was my low self-esteem. By hearing a few of my past experiences you can develop a sense of why I wasn't developing a positive body image. I had a fear of becoming fat and perceived myself as never being thin enough. In my mind if you wanted to be loved, you had to be thin. Every time I'd lose a few pounds I would feel like I was worthy of love and friendships, but whenever I would gain a few pounds, I felt like a failure and not worthy of love and friendships. My moods and how I felt about myself were directly related to my body's weight gain or loss.

The best way I can explain how I felt is by saying that there was a battle raging inside of me. Being a perfectionist at everything I did became important, and trying to figure out where I fit in became an obsession. I wanted to be accepted by others my own age, and I didn't want to be a disappointment to my parents. These were two factors that I had no control over and I felt I wasn't accomplishing.

My eating habits, which I still didn't know at this point had a diagnostic name, were a way to cope with my feelings of inadequacy. It was one thing in my life that I could control. It became a part of my identity in high school. It was the one thing that I felt I had control over and no one could take away from me.

There are three factors in my high school experience that I have to tell you about. They are important, because they had an impact on my life and are essential in understanding how I overcame my eating disorder. The three important factors are meeting Scott, Patrick, and learning that my eating behavior had a diagnostic name. We must go back in time to my first day of high school at Effingham, Kansas.

Dad drove me to the nearest bus stop so I could catch the bus to my new school. I'll have to admit that I was nervous about starting all over again in high school. The school was about twenty-five to thirty minutes away. My parents decided I'd have to ride the bus until I could get a driver's license and drive myself.

"Are you okay, Courteney? You look a little nervous," Dad asked.

"I'll be fine, Dad. I am nervous, but very excited about being in high school," I replied feeling butterflies fluttering around in my stomach.

"Everything will get better at this school, Courteney," Dad replied.

I knew he was trying to make me feel better. I appreciated his kindness.

Smiling, I jokingly replied, "Well, it couldn't get much worse. I will be just fine. Don't worry, Dad."

I could see a bus coming down the dirt road. I knew it was probably the bus I was waiting for.

"See you later, Dad. Love you," I said stepping out of the car.

It was a beautiful, cool fall day. I couldn't have asked for a more perfect day. The bus opened its doors and I stepped into a long, yellow bus that had maybe a dozen students aboard.

"Hi there, honey," the bus driver cheerfully stated giving me a big smile. "Sit wherever you like. There's plenty of room."

"Thank you," I replied smiling back at her. I started to sit down in the first seat when someone in the very back of the bus started yelling something towards the front.

"Come sit back here," hollered a guy from the back of the bus.

I wasn't sure what to say or do, so I just looked at the bus driver. Maybe she could help me out.

"That's my son. Go ahead and move to the back if you like and talk with him," she said smiling.

I headed down the aisle to the very back of the bus. The guy scooted over and patted the seat signaling for me to sit next to him. My first impression of him was that he was cute. He had dark, curly hair and a welcoming smile. The butterflies in my stomach were fluttering faster than ever as I sat down next to him in the seat.

"Hi! My name is Patrick. Patrick Dooley. What's your name?" he asked.

"Courteney... Courteney Baker."

"You're new aren't you? Where are you from?"

"I'm from Atchison. I use to go to school there, but decided to transfer out to Effingham schools."

"Great. I'm officially your first new friend," he said giving me one of his handsome smiles.

I knew I was going to like Patrick from the moment I met him. My first bus ride to my new school flew by quickly while I sat there talking with Patrick.

When we arrived at the school I walked in with Patrick. He showed me to the office, and then he took off down the hallway. I hoped that I would see him again today. The secretary was very nice and had my schedule ready.

"I'll show you where your locker is and walk you to your first class," she said with a smile.

"Thanks," I replied following her down the long hallway.

I could feel people staring at me. It wasn't a bad kind of stare, just the kind you get when everyone is curious who you are. My locker was next to the back doors of the school. The locker was smaller than I was use to, but it would do. She gave me my combination, and I quickly opened it and threw in my jacket. The bell had already rung so I knew we needed to hurry to first class.

I glanced at my schedule and saw that I had English first hour with Mr. Tyler. I wasn't crazy about starting my day with English. It wasn't my favorite subject. I enjoyed writing and reading books, but breaking down a sentence into predicates, subjects, nouns, and verbs was unpleasant. It just wasn't what I called having fun. English was difficult for me, but I knew I had to take it.

The secretary, Mrs. Blair, stopped in front of a classroom and signaled to the teacher that I was here.

"Mr. Tyler is your teacher and will get you started for the day," stated Mrs. Blair.

"Thank you for your help," I replied.

I stepped into the classroom and saw all eyes go on me. How I hated to be the center of attention and the new kid in school.

"Hello," said Mr. Tyler with a warm smile. "There are two seats in the room vacant. Take your pick."

I immediately started scanning the room for the two vacant desks. One was in the back row, and the other was in the front row. Normally, I would choose the desk in the back, but something about the front row seat caught my attention. I walked nervously to the front row seat and quickly sat down.

"What is your name?" asked Mr. Tyler.

"Courteney...Courteney Baker," I replied barely able to get the words out.

"We have a lot to do in class today, but we'll take the last fifteen minutes to introduce ourselves to Courteney," stated Mr. Tyler.

How I wished that Patrick was in this class so at least I would know one person. I had enjoyed talking with Patrick on the way to school. There was something about him that made me feel comfortable and at ease. He was easy to talk to and made me forget about being a ball of nerves. This was a freshman English class, and Patrick was a sophomore. I wasn't sure how many classes I would have with him, but I hoped I might at least have one.

Mr. Tyler went on with his English lecture, but I can't say I heard much of it. I just couldn't concentrate on what he was talking about because of being nervous.

The one thing that did catch my attention about the front row seat was the guy sitting behind me. I noticed him immediately when I was scanning the room looking for a vacant seat. When I first saw him his eyes caught my attention. He had the most beautiful, big, brown eyes. There was something mysterious and breathtaking about them. Maybe I would get a chance to speak with him at the end of class.

"Why don't we take some time now to introduce ourselves to Courteney," stated Mr. Tyler after finishing his lecture.

I was anxious to hear everyone's name, maybe I might know someone. Everyone introduced themselves by name, but I recognized none of them. I did pay close attention to the guy's name that was sitting behind me. His name was Scott Linwood. By the way he had his head down when he introduced himself, he appeared to be shy towards girls. His hair was a brownish auburn color and complimented his dark brown eyes. I thought he was one of the most gorgeous guys I had ever seen.

After introductions, Mr. Tyler told us we could talk for the remaining time. I wasn't the best at talking to people I didn't know, but I wanted to make new friends and hoped that this school would be a better experience. Everyone in class was nice and made me feel comfortable. The guy behind me, Scott, didn't speak a word. That was the one person in class I wanted to talk to. I finally got up the nerve to speak to him.

Turning around in my chair I smiled and said, "Hi." His eyes locked with mine for a few seconds.

"Hi," he replied.

I could tell he was on the shy side. If I wanted conversation with him I was going to have to do the talking.

"Do you live here in Effingham?" I asked smiling at him.

"No, I live in Cummings," he replied nervously.

"Do you play football?" I asked knowing it was football season.

"No, but I'm on the wrestling team," he replied relaxing a bit.

I could tell he was beginning to relax. We didn't get to talk long before the bell rang for second hour.

As the days of high school went by, I learned to love Patrick and

Scott. My love for them was different, but yet the same in a sense. My love for Scott was in a romantic way and for Patrick in a brotherly way. Yet my love for each was equally important in my life.

Scott and I dated off and on in high school. We were totally in love for a few months, then would break up and take a break for a while. We both dated other people during our break ups, but I always felt a part of me was missing when I wasn't with him. Somehow our love for one another always managed to pull us back together.

Patrick and I were best friends. We had other friends of the same gender too, but we had a special relationship. We always made time for one another, and I loved our long talks we had about our dreams. He knew more about me than anyone else. The only thing he didn't know about me was my eating behavior. That was a secret I was willing to share with no one. So many times I wanted to tell him, but feared I would lose him as a friend if I did.

I had continued to practice this behavior about one to two times a week. It wasn't until my sophomore year in health class that I found out my eating behavior had a diagnostic name. We were reading out loud in class about eating disorders. When the section on bulimia nervosa was read aloud, it took everything I had to hide my fear and hold back the tears. This is what it said:

> An eating disorder is a complex psychological illness characterized by a distorted body image, an intense fear of gaining weight, and an obsession with food. Bulimia nervosa involves eating large amounts of food within a short period (bingeing) and then purging the food by vomiting or using enemas, laxatives or diuretics. Many people with this disorder also exercise compulsively. Between the bingeing and purging episodes, people with bulimia nervosa usually restrict how much they eat. People with eating disorders seem to be preoccupied with weight and body image.
>
> Feelings of disgust or shame related to the illness can trigger further bulimic episodes, leading to the development of a vicious cycle. People who have buli-

mia nervosa often maintain a normal weight but may
engage in frequent eating binges—eating huge quanti-
ties of food in one sitting. Between binges, many fast
excessively. Because many women who have bulimia
are of normal weight, the disorder often is unnoticed
by family and friends. Bulimia nervosa has serious consequences and can be life-threatening.

It felt like my heart had sunk into the pit of my stomach when I
read this information on eating disorders. I couldn't believe what I
had just learned. I had an eating disorder. How could this happen?
I started making excuses for my behavior and tried to convince
myself that I had everything under control. If I did have an eating
disorder, I wouldn't let it get out of control. I could stop whenever
I wanted to; I just didn't want to yet. I had lost some weight and
was getting along great in school.

By the end of my junior year in high school I had enough cred-
its to graduate. I was all for graduating a year early. Patrick was
a senior and would be graduating and going to Kansas University in Lawrence, Kansas. His dream was to become a doctor, and
there was no doubt in my mind that he would succeed. I hadn't
figured out yet what I wanted to get my degree in, but I knew that
I wanted to be at Kansas University with Patrick.

Scott and I were still dating off and on. More on than off. We
were both crazy about each other. Scott still had one more year
of high school. I hated to graduate before him. Not getting to see
him everyday would drive me crazy, but he promised to come and
see me in Lawrence. It wasn't that far from his home. He had plans
of joining the military after high school, and I just wasn't sure
where that would leave us as a couple.

Kelli was also graduating from high school and planning on
going to Kansas University with her boyfriend, Dylan. I can't say
I'm totally thrilled with the idea of having my older sister there
watching over me. I knew she'd probably watch every move I made
and wouldn't agree with anything I ever did. Our relationship had
changed very little through high school. I was still never allowed
to touch her belongings or to enter her room. I wanted to feel

close to her, but I wasn't sure how to improve our relationship. It seemed to me that I was always wrong, and she always knew best.

John still struggled in school and fitting into society. He wanted so much to be everyone's friend, but not all wanted to be his friend. He knew he was different than others, and it bothered him. I wish I knew the right things to say to help him feel better about himself, but I just didn't. I loved John dearly, but it was hard to have a close relationship with him. I longed to have a sibling that I could feel close to, and Patrick filled that spot in my heart.

I was seventeen and going off to college. I would be living in an apartment just off campus. I was excited and nervous all at once. Being out of my parents' house would make it easier to hide my bulimia. I knew that if I continued my eating disorder it could result in death. I knew my mother would be horrified and never send me off to college if she found out her daughter could end up dead from an eating disorder she knew nothing about. I told myself that once I got to college I would stop bingeing and purging. I just knew I could stop this behavior on my own and no one would ever have to find out.

Lawrence, Kansas 1985–1986, *Hitting Rock Bottom*

I shut the door of my new, one-bedroom apartment and plopped myself down on the used black vinyl couch my parents had purchased. I had said my good-byes to them after a long day of moving my belongings and setting up my apartment for college. It was a hot, sticky, summer day in July, and I was exhausted from the heat of the day. I could already tell I wasn't going to like the vinyl couch. It was one of those that your skin stuck to, especially when you were sweaty.

I was thrilled about living in an apartment. I didn't want to live in the college dorms, and amazingly my parents agreed to let me stay in an apartment as long as I had a roommate. My roommate, Joy, was older, in her last year of college, and had a serious boyfriend that lived out of town. I knew she probably wouldn't be around much, which would give me the privacy I wanted. Even though there was a big age difference between Joy and me, we got along well. I had met Joy when I was on the dance team at Atchison Junior High. She choreographed the dances. She was an excellent dancer and loved to exercise as much as I did.

I needed to find a job so I would have some spending money. Our apartment building, The Oaks, sat right on a main strip of town that had lots of restaurants. I wanted to find a job that could be walking distance in case I didn't have the car. My sister and I would be sharing a vehicle that mom and dad left for us. Kelli was living on campus in the dorms, so I knew I wouldn't always have the car accessible to me. I had noticed that there was a small donut shop directly across the street. I thought I'd start there and work my way down the street.

I was tired, but my adrenaline was flowing from all the excitement. I still couldn't believe I had my own place. It was a small, one bedroom, one bath apartment, but I thought it was wonderful. For me it meant having some freedom and making some of my own choices. I was in charge of my days and evenings without parents watching over my every move.

I swiftly rose up off the couch and headed for the bathroom. I wanted to get cleaned up a bit before I went to the donut shop to apply for a job.

Stopping in front of the large, full-view bathroom mirror, I didn't like what I saw. All I could see was a girl who had so many imperfections, who wasn't doing the best she could. I wanted to turn my life around and put a stop to my eating disorder. I wasn't off to a good start though. I hadn't eaten anything for almost two days now, due to a bingeing and purging episode.

My throat always was hurting and I was constantly sucking on lozenges. My stomach had been cramping all day letting me know I needed to eat something, but to be honest I was afraid to eat. I always start off with good intentions of eating a healthy meal, then somehow I just lose control and end up eating thousands of calories and the bingeing, purging, and fasting cycle starts all over again.

How was I going to get my eating disorder under control and figure out what I wanted to do with my life? I hadn't figured out the answer yet, but somehow I was going to stop this craziness. I wanted to feel better, and I wanted to be in control. First, I needed a job and a good meal. I quickly cleaned up and headed out the door.

I heard Joy stirring around in the kitchen and knew that she was preparing herself for another day on campus. I reached down and pulled the soft blanket up closely around me. How I wanted to stay there all day. I knew that I should be up preparing for my classes too, but I felt so ill. I didn't know if I had enough energy to even pull myself out of bed.

The fall semester had flown by, and the spring semester only had a couple months left. I lay there in bed for a few minutes looking around the room and thinking about the last eight months. Tears starting burning my eyes and rolling down my cheeks.

I had failed miserably at getting my life straightened out. It seemed like failure was my middle name. My parents were highly disappointed in my grades, and my eating disorder had grown worse. Keeping my grades acceptable was a challenge with being so sick all the time. I made an effort to go to class, but many times, even if I was present, I couldn't concentrate on what was being said by the instructor.

One positive aspect that had changed in my life was I began to realize that I needed God. The only person I shared my secret with was God. I have noticed numerous posters on campus about church groups and wanting people to join their congregation. One poster in particular caught my attention. It said, "Talk to God, he will listen. He is forgiving and loves all!" More than ever I wanted to walk into a church and talk with someone who knew more about God's love.

My problem was that I was still too afraid to walk into a church and become a member of their congregation. I wasn't used to going to church, and it made me feel uncomfortable. My fear was being laughed at by other members. I knew nothing about the bible and was afraid they would see that and laugh me right out the door.

I knew I had a long way to go in my inner growth, in learning to trust my life to God. "Lord, I'm listening and watching for signs. Please speak to me and help me, please. I don't know who else to turn to," I whispered into the silence of the room.

Turning my attention to the clock on the nightstand, I realized I was going to be late for my psychology class. Somehow I managed to pull myself out of bed and get ready for class.

I stepped off the campus bus and headed for the student union. My psychology class was in the big auditorium. The campus was beautiful this time of year. It was springtime and the bright green buds on the trees and shrubs were showing their beauty. My English professor was talking about spring being the time of rebirth. People all around me seemed to be enjoying the beauty of springtime, but I just couldn't seem to feel that happiness and enjoy the beauty of it all.

"Courteney, wait up," shouted Patrick crossing the street.

"Hi, Patrick, where are you headed?"

"I'm headed to class. You don't look so good, are you okay?"

"Just not feeling well. I was awake most of the night with headaches."

I hated lying to Patrick, but there was no way I could tell him I had three bingeing and purging episodes yesterday.

"Are you taking your medicine the doctor prescribed for you?"

"No, I told you I didn't want to take that medicine anymore. It makes me feel so tired all the time."

"Well you're sick all the time anyway. What's the difference?"

"My body will eventually adjust, and I'll get better. Trust me."

Patrick put his arms around me and held me tight. It was one of those warm and lingering hugs that gave you warm fuzzies.

"I love you, Courteney. I don't want anything to happen to you."

"I love you too, Patrick. I'm going to be okay."

"I'm going to come by tonight and check on you. Are you going to be home?"

"Yes, but I have to work early in the morning at the donut shop. I can't stay up too late."

Giving me a kiss on the forehead, we said our good-byes and headed to class.

It tore at my heart to be dishonest with Patrick. I wanted so much to tell him the truth, but was just too scared. All Patrick knew was that I had taken myself off my childhood medicine that helped prevent migraines. I hated taking it as a child, because it did make me feel tired all the time. The doctors also said I wouldn't be able to have children while taking this medicine. I always told him that my body was just trying to adjust going off the medicine. Part of it was the truth. I had taken myself off the medicine that I had taken for over ten years. My not feeling well was due more to my bulimia nervosa than taking myself off the medicine.

"Hi, Courteney," said Kelli coming down the stairs.

"Hi, Kelli."

"Where are you going?"

"I'm headed to psychology class. I need to hurry. See you later," I said heading up the stairs as fast as I could to avoid her.

We were getting along better now in college, but I wasn't in the mood to answer fifty questions. She was more like little mother hen to me than a sister.

It took everything I had to make it through psychology class. With my stomach aching, throat sore, and sleep trying to take my body over I didn't comprehend much of what the professor said. My grade in class reflected my efforts. I knew I'd be in big trouble with my parents when they saw my grades again this semester.

After class I headed straight for the campus bathroom that had a big, soft couch. It was calling me, and I ended up sleeping there for the rest of the day.

When I arrived back home, I showered and tried to look half-way decent. Patrick would be over soon, and I didn't want him worrying about me. My entire body ached and the mere thought of food made me feel sick to my stomach. I hadn't eaten anything since my last bingeing and purging episode, and I probably wouldn't for at least another twenty-four hours.

When Patrick arrived he had a bottle of wine and some popcorn. One of our favorite things to do together was to eat popcorn, drink wine, and watch the show, "Bosom Buddies." Unfortunately, there was no way I could eat anything. My stomach was in too much discomfort. I was a pro at making up excuses and just told him I had already eaten and couldn't possibly eat another bite. He had no reason to believe otherwise and didn't think much of my excuse.

We had one of our long talks that I always enjoy. Many times I would just sit back and let Patrick do all the talking. He had his future clearly planned and knew exactly what he wanted in life. He was handsome, kind hearted, and would make a wonderful doctor. His future looked promising, and I knew he would accomplish every goal he set his mind to. I envied him. It must be a relief to know exactly what you want to do with your life.

He didn't stay long. We watched our show, and then I headed to bed. To be at work by four in the morning was a challenge. I knew I needed to get some sleep, or I'd never make it to work.

That night as I lay in bed, I thought about what I wanted to say in my prayer. I made a promise to myself that I would at least say a prayer once a day. I wasn't even sure if I knew how to pray correctly. If there was a correct way, I knew I was probably not doing it right. It seemed to me that I didn't do a lot of things correctly. I wanted to be a better person, and I wanted to please the people I loved the most. My life was becoming a huge collection of lies. I hated this, and I knew I needed to make things right. If I told the truth about my illness, I would disappoint and hurt a lot of people. Shame and embarrassment were also playing a factor in not wanting people to know about my illness.

I laid my head back against my pillow and a tear slowly ran down my cheek. "Lord, please help me. Please help me sort out all of my problems and feelings so I can do the right thing. I feel so much shame, and I don't know how to make that go away. Are you listening, Lord? Please let me know you are listening."

Morning had come and I was feeling a little better. I managed to get to work, and I had made a promise to myself that I would try to eat at least one healthy meal today. It was Saturday, and Scott was supposed to come down for the weekend to spend time with me. We were still dating off and on and enjoyed spending time with each other when we could.

I was deeply in love with Scott and hoped that one day we would get married. We had conversations once in a while about getting married, but the talk was more if we got married. He hadn't proposed marriage, and I was still uncertain where our relationship was headed if he joined the military and was shipped off to another state or perhaps even another country.

My parents weren't crazy about the idea of Scott and me getting serious. They liked him, but I have heard many times from them that Scott and I are two different people. We come from different kinds of families. My parents both have a college education and have gone to graduate school. Scott's parents had a high school education. They had dreams of their daughter getting a higher education and marrying someone with similar goals. Scott didn't have an interest in college, and truthfully I didn't care. He was a hard worker, and I knew that we could make it work.

By the time my shift ended at work I was starving. Patrick had stopped by and asked if I wanted to have lunch with him. I accepted his invitation. Patrick had a car and offered to drive. We went to a small pub downtown. I reminded myself of the promise I made, and ordered a chicken salad sandwich with fresh fruit. Every bite I took was painful to swallow, but I managed to eat it all without Patrick noticing my difficulty.

"How are you feeling today, Courteney?" Patrick asked with concern in his eyes.

"I'm feeling much better."

"Do you have any plans for this weekend? I'm going out on a date tonight. You can always come along. We might go to the movies."

"Thanks for the offer, but Scott is coming down for the weekend. Maybe we can go to the movies another time. Anyway, I doubt your date wants a tag along," I said smiling teasingly at him.

He was always inviting me along on his dates. I think he just didn't want me to be alone or feel left out. Our world that we shared was one of love and compassion. He was always looking out for me, and I appreciated his thoughtfulness.

When I arrived back at my apartment the phone was ringing as I stepped through the door. It was Scott. He was canceling our plans for the weekend. He had a family reunion to attend and wouldn't be able to come down. We were both disappointed. It seemed that lately we haven't had much alone time.

It was great when he could come down for an entire weekend.

We usually spent our time together going to the movies. We both enjoyed a good action movie. It took my mind off of my troubles. Scott had a way of making me feel alive inside. We were two different people, but very much in love.

I could call Patrick and go with him to the movies, but I knew his date wouldn't appreciate me being along. He always introduced me as his sister, but you could always tell the girl never appreciated me being on their date. My roommate was also gone for the weekend which left me alone.

I decided I would do some reading and get caught up on some of my classes. I had good intentions of reading, but sleep soon found me. It was more of a nap. I awoke after a couple hours of sleep, and I knew immediately where my evening was headed. I was starving, my body was shaking, and I felt out of control. I hated this feeling, and I knew what it meant.

I walked across the street to the grocery store and bought tons of junk food and a box of laxatives. Laxatives were something I had started when I arrived at college. I was never sure if I purged all of the food out of my stomach, and was afraid of gaining weight. I figured the laxatives would help clean out my stomach. I usually would take four or five laxatives after an episode.

When I arrived back at my apartment with my supplies I started bingeing. I felt in total control until I started purging. It's like all the life in you is being drained out of you. Extreme weakness and tiredness overcame me, and I needed to sleep.

For some reason taking four or five laxatives tonight wasn't enough. My entire body shook from uncontrollable sobs. I took five, then another five, then another five, until I took the entire box. I fell to the floor crying uncontrollably suddenly realizing the full extent of what I had just done. I had just taken an entire box of laxatives. I knew this couldn't be good, but truthfully I didn't care anymore. I was tired of being sick and feeling like I was disappointing everybody I loved.

I laid myself down in bed and said my nightly prayer. I fell asleep whispering, "Lord, please let my parents, Kelli, John, Scott, and Patrick know that I love them. I'm sorry for all the pain and disappointment I have caused. I'm tired of being sick and I don't

know how to make it better. I want to come and be with you, Lord.
Please let me be free of pain."

Moving Away

Katie came running to me with a huge bear hug. "Hi, Courteney," she squealed with delight, "I've missed you so much."

"I've missed you too, Katie," I said giving her a hug and kiss. How I missed my little Katie while I was away at college. She was the little neighbor girl that I babysat when I was in junior high and high school. She was just a tiny baby when I first held her in my arms. Now at seven, she was growing into her girlhood. Her brown hair, hazel eyes, darling smile, and bubbly personality made her a breathtaking little girl.

"You've grown taller. You weren't supposed to do any growing while I was away," I said giving her a teasing smile. "You're as beautiful as ever."

She stood on tiptoes and gave me a soft kiss on the left cheek. "I'm glad you're home, Courteney. I'm going shopping with mom, but I'll be over again to see you. Maybe we can bake some cookies." That was Katie's favorite thing to do when I babysat.

"That would be great, Katie. Have fun shopping with your mom. Tell her I said hello. When you come back I want to hear all about school." Before I could say anymore, Katie was running home waving to me all the way.

I was thankful to still be here to enjoy my little Katie's hugs and kisses. After taking an entire box of laxatives, I wasn't sure if I would make it. For three days I was extremely sick, and at times wondered if I was going to be here the next day. Each morning though, I would wake up still lying in bed. I prayed a lot, probably more than I had ever in my life. Was there a reason for me still being here? I wasn't sure how to answer that question, but I knew that I would never take an entire box of laxatives again.

What Katie didn't know was that I wouldn't be home for very long. In a few days I was heading to Woodbury, Connecticut, to be a nanny. My first year at college didn't go well. My eating disorder had grown worse, and my grades suffered so severely that I was put on the probation list.

My parents weren't pleased with my academic performance. I can't say I blame them for being upset. If I was putting out money for my child's education, and they weren't giving it their all, I'd be upset too. My father had told me to get a job and find another place to live. It saddened me to know that I was disappointing and hurting so many people.

My solution, whether right or wrong, was to move away. I didn't want to live at home with my parents anymore, and I knew I couldn't afford a place on my own. It wasn't because I felt they were awful parents, but it was more my drive to be independent.

One day on campus, I had come across an ad in the school newspaper about nanny jobs on the east coast. I saved the number thinking it sounded interesting. I love to travel, a trait I get from my father, had a love for children, and usually had no problem with getting home sick.

Scott had graduated from high school and enlisted in the military. He was going to be stationed at Fort Hood in Killeen, Texas. This was going to put a lot of miles between him and me, but I felt I needed to get away.

Scott and I had made plans to get married the next year. I would spend one year as a nanny, and then move to Texas with him. My two goals, while living in Connecticut, were to save money to help us start out in our marriage and to get my eating disorder under control. It would be harder to binge and purge while living in someone else's house. I would be responsible for a five year old little girl and knew that would keep me busy.

The next three days flew by quickly with packing and saying my good-byes. I kept my promise to Katie and baked chocolate chip cookies with her at my parents' house. She was excited and talked about school and friends nonstop. She was a typical little girl who loved to jabber. My heart broke when I had to tell her I was moving away again. I was going to miss her so much. Her spirits lifted though when I told her about Scott and I getting married. We wanted her to be a candle lighter in our wedding. She thought Scott was the cutest and loved it when he came over. She always told me she was going to find a Scott of her own someday.

My last night with my family was typical. Mom fixed dinner for the family, and dad sat at the bar having his peanuts and mixed drinks. I often wonder if dad will ever get tired of drinking that nasty smelling substance. I have my doubts. He is pretty set in his ways.

"Dinner is great, mom. Thanks for making one of my favorite dinners before I leave tomorrow." Mom made the best chicken and dumplings.

"You're welcome, Courteney. It was my pleasure," she said with a warm smile.

"Are you excited about living in Connecticut?" asked John excitedly.

"Yes, I am. I think I'll like the east coast."

"Do you really think you need to eat all that food, Randi? All it's going to do is make you big. You know I don't like big women," Dad stated with sarcasm in his voice.

I pushed the chair back from the dining room table and excused myself from dinner. Dad always had a way of ruining a nice family dinner with his unwise comments.

"Thanks for dinner, Mom. It was great. I have a big day tomorrow and want to get to bed early. Goodnight everyone," I said quickly heading to my room.

I wasn't going to miss hearing dad's intolerable comments. It saddened me to hear him talk that way to mom. It shouldn't matter how big or small she is. I knew if I said anything to him I would be scolded and told I was being disrespectful. Knowing I couldn't say or do anything to make the situation better, I prepared myself for bed.

I quietly walked into Krista's bedroom to see if she had fallen asleep. Brushing a soft strand of her brown hair back off her face, I softly kissed her right cheek. What a beautiful little girl I had been blessed with and allowed to be her nanny. The last ten months with the Zimmerman family had gone quickly, and I had fallen in love with another precious little girl. How I would miss her when I left in the fall to get married.

Krista had turned five since I had come to take care of her and was in kindergarten. She kept me busy with school activities and swimming lessons. I enjoyed spending time with her. She was a well behaved little girl that was very loveable.

Her parents, Peter and Bette, were equally as wonderful. I was fortunate to get such a magnificent family. They took me into their home and treated me just like I was their own daughter. I had met other nannies that hadn't been as fortunate as me and received families that treated them like hired help.

Bette was working on her doctor's degree in psychology, and Peter owned an insurance business. Between Bette working full-time at the University of Connecticut and working on her doctrine, there were times when she didn't have much time for the family. But when she did have extra time away from work and studies, she always made a point to spend time with her daughter. You could feel the unconditional love she had for her daughter, and Krista was a mirror image of her mother.

Peter reminded me of my own father in some aspects. He was the carefree "let's go out and do something fun today" kind of guy. Every Saturday morning Krista, Peter, and I would go to McDonald's for breakfast and then do the weekly grocery shopping. After the groceries were put away, there was usually some kind of adventure for the afternoon. Swimming at the country club or the lake was a favorite. Peter was a good swimmer and competed from time to time. He was athletic, and swimming was his passion that he could share with his daughter. Krista was always ecstatic when she spent time with her father.

My eating disorder was a little better, but still very much a problem. Bette had recognized that my eating habits weren't great and had several talks with me about eating healthy. She hadn't figured out that I was bulimic but was suspicious about my behaviors at times. She was always patient with me and listened to what I had to say. I wanted to tell her the truth so many times, but just didn't have the nerve to do it. Since she was a psychologist, it would've been the perfect person to confess to. I wasn't ready to reveal my secret though. My eating habits had become addictive and very much a part of me. I was good at hiding my bingeing and purging episodes and felt when I was ready to stop I could.

"Courteney. Are you asleep?" Krista said tiptoeing into my bedroom.

"No, I'm not asleep, Krista. Come on in."

"I can't sleep. Will you tell me a story?"

"Sure I will," I said giving her a hug. "Let's go to your room and curl up in your bed."

Krista loved to hear stories at bedtime. Her favorite was Cinderella. She never tired of hearing this story, and loved the part when Cinderella goes to the formal ball in a beautiful white gown.

"I'm going to go to a ball someday, and I'll wear a beautiful gown just like Cinderella," Krista said sleepily.

"You'll be the prettiest girl at the ball too. You know that?"

"Will you tell me the story again?"

"No, Krista—once is enough. You need to get some sleep. We have a big day tomorrow. We're going to your grandma's house for Easter dinner."

I tucked the blankets snug around her little body and gave her a kiss on the forehead.

"I love you, Krista. See you in the morning."

"I love you too, Courteney," she said yawning and closing her eyes.

Peter and Bette's bedroom was right next to Krista's. The light on Bette's night stand was still glowing. I knew she was still up reading. Bette was dedicated to her job and doctoral studies.

"Goodnight, Bette," I whispered.

"Goodnight, Courteney. See you in the morning."

I was tired after our adventure to the local amusement park and my daily jog. I was jogging five miles a day now. I wasn't fast, but I had a steady pace. I didn't care about being a slow jogger; my goal was to burn as many calories as possible.

If I jogged five miles, then I allowed myself five pieces of fruit and vegetables a day. Today I had eaten three apples and two oranges. It wasn't much to keep your energy level up, but somehow I always managed. The fact that I hadn't binged or purged for two days now made me feel great. I hated these episodes, and they always made me feel so tired.

Snuggling under the warm blankets, my thoughts wandered to what tomorrow would bring. We were having a full course Easter dinner at Peter's parents' house. His mother was widowed and was a lovely lady. You would never know I wasn't one of her grandchildren. I enjoyed visiting with her, but the dinner is what made me nervous. I wasn't comfortable with eating around other people and was always self conscious about what I ate. There would be a huge layout of delicious foods; most of them I wouldn't allow myself to eat.

I leaned over to turn on the radio on my nightstand. Hearing the phone ring in the distance, I wondered who would be calling at this late of hour. I wasn't planning on moving from my cozy spot in bed, and knew Bette was still up. She would probably answer the phone at this late of an hour.

Closing my eyes, I started to think about what I wanted to say in my prayer.

"Courteney... Courteney. Are you awake?" Bette whispered from my doorway.

Opening my eyes, I saw Bette standing near me with the phone in her hand. Immediately, I could tell something was wrong.

"Yes, I'm awake. What's the matter?" I said feeling a lump forming in my throat.

Bette sat down on the bed next to me and handed me the phone saying, "Your mother wants to speak with you."

I reached for the phone feeling there was something terribly wrong. My first instinct was something had happened to my brother.

"Hello," I spoke softly into the receiver.

"Courteney... Courteney, I have something to tell you that

is going to upset you. Is Bette still there with you?" asked my mother.

"Yes," I replied softly. Tears were already pooling into my eyes. I could feel something was terribly wrong.

"I don't know how to tell you this, so I guess I'll just say it. Patrick was killed in an automobile accident last night. I'm so sorry, Courteney."

She went on to say more, but I didn't hear any of it. My heart felt like it had been ripped out, and my entire body felt numb. I couldn't believe what I had just heard.

"Courteney... Courteney are you still there? Are you okay?"

"Yes, I'm still here. I need to go, mom," I could barely whisper the words.

"Courteney... I am so sorry. I know how much you love Patrick."

"I'll talk with you later. Bye."

Hanging up the phone, I just sat there staring at the wall. I had totally forgotten that Bette was sitting next to me on the bed.

This couldn't be true. How could God allow such a good person to die at such a young age? His birthday was the day before mine. He had just turned twenty years old, and I was nineteen now. We had spoken on the phone over our birthdays. We shared information about our lives, and his last words were, "I love you, Courteney. Don't ever forget how much I love you."

"I love you too, Patrick. I'll call you again soon," I stated lovingly.

He still had a lifetime ahead of him, and so much going for him. He was intelligent, musically talented, and most importantly I loved him with all my heart. I just couldn't understand how this could happen. I felt my body starting to tremble, and the wet tears burning my cheeks. Bette's arms went around me, and I cried until sleep finally found me.

With a trembling body, I lay back against my pillow and stared at the framed picture of Patrick and me on my dresser. This was one of my favorite photographs of us, and it reflected our youthful age.

Patrick's naturally curly brown hair and his soft smile kept him looking young. I knew as he grew into his manhood his features would compliment him.

The photograph was taken one evening about two years ago when we were getting ready to go to a rock concert in Kansas City. We were standing outside of Kemper Arena, and had asked a stranger walking by to take our picture. We had our arms around one another, and I had laid my head on his chest. After the stranger had taken our picture, they gave us a warm smile and told us we made a darling couple.

Patrick had said, "Thanks, but this is my younger sister."

"Lord, why Patrick? He had so much to give. I just don't understand."

I pulled the blankets up closer to me trying to stop the cold chill I felt throughout my entire body. I didn't want to attend the Easter dinner today or be around anyone. All I wanted to do was curl up in bed and remember the wonderful memories that Patrick and I had shared. Maybe I would even be able to sleep until all of the pain went away. I had never lost a loved one before, and the unbearable hurt that goes with it was a new experience for me.

"Courteney... Courteney, are you awake?" whispered Bette.

I didn't say a word for fear I would start crying again. I just looked at her. She had brought me a glass of orange juice.

"I know it is hard when you lose a loved one, Courteney, but you will feel better if you get up and try to move around a little bit. Why don't you take a shower and get cleaned up. We want you with us today for Easter."

"Okay... just give me a minute."

Sitting the juice on my nightstand, Bette said, "I'm here for you whenever you need someone to talk to."

Trying to show my appreciation with a small grin, but failing miserably by allowing more tears to flow, I managed to get out a, "Thanks."

Somehow I managed to pull myself out of bed and get ready for Easter dinner. My appetite was nonexistent, but I did manage to drink a little at Bette's request. I didn't want to spoil everyone's Easter, but it was very difficult to even get through the day. Everyone insisted I be there even though I told them I wouldn't be great company.

By the time we arrived back home, it felt like my body had been through a war zone. My emotions were up and down from sobbing uncontrollably to sitting there quietly staring off into space. At times I couldn't even feel my emotions due to the numbness that overtook my body.

Several days went by, and Bette stayed right by my side. I don't know what I would've done without her. She was getting worried, because I hadn't eaten in several days.

"You know, Courteney, maybe you would feel better if you prayed and talked to Patrick. Let him know that you are going to be okay without him. Even though he is absent from you in body, he can be present with you always in spirit," she said giving me a hug of encouragement.

"Do you really think he will hear me if I talk to him? I've never lost anyone before, and I don't know how to do this. Will you stay with me and help me?" I asked wiping away the tears that were falling freely.

"Of course he will hear you, Courteney. God will help you get through your pain. Both of them will listen. I'm sure Patrick needs to know that you will be all right. Come sit next to me, and I'll be with you while you pray."

I sat next to Bette and for a while could do nothing but stare at the floor trying to put my thoughts and emotions in order.

Quietly I prayed, "Lord, please help me get through the pain of losing Patrick. He meant the world to me, and I need for him to know that. I don't know if he can hear me Lord, but please let him know that I love him and that I will be okay," wiping away my tears I went on, "Patrick, I will never forget you. You will always be in my heart, and I have the special memories of times we have shared. I will never let go of those memories. I love you, Patrick—Amen."

There was an amazing feeling of warmth and security that washed through my body. Somehow I knew that everything would be okay, but it would take time.

Tucking me into my bed, Bette asked, "Do you feel better, Courteney?"

"Yes...yes, Bette. Thank you so much for everything."

"You're welcome. Now get some rest. I'll make a nice breakfast in the morning."

"That would be great. Goodnight."

I laid in bed thinking about everything that had happened in the past few days. The tears still fell nonstop, and I wondered if I would ever stop crying.

It is strange how everything can change so quickly. I had been trying to pray more in the past year in hopes of developing a better relationship with God. I didn't blame God for Patrick's death, and I knew I needed Him in my life more than ever now. God was the answer to getting through this difficult time, and the immeasurable pain I was feeling.

I stared at the crescent moon through the sliding glass door in my bedroom. I wondered where Patrick was and what he was doing. I've always believed and known there was a heaven, but it was like a magical place in my mind. It still was a magical, wonderful place to me, but much more now than before. I had lost Patrick, who I deeply loved. I would miss him more than words could describe, but heaven gave me hope that our relationship was not over. Some day I would see him again.

A Blessing from God

I stood in front of the full-view mirror rubbing my swollen hands over my enlarged round belly. I could feel our baby moving around inside, stretching and kicking his tiny feet up into my right rib. I gently pushed his foot down and reassured our baby boy that he would soon be coming out to meet his parents that loved him so very much.

"You have to wait until your father gets home from Korea before you can come out little one," I said stroking the sides of my belly that felt hard as a rock.

The last eight months had been difficult going through a pregnancy without my husband, but I had managed and was looking forward to picking him up from the Kansas City International Airport today.

Scott and I were married on October 3, 1987, in Atchison, Kansas, at the Trinity Episcopal Church. This was also the church where my mother was a full-time organist. Mom was exceptionally talented at playing the organ.

My sister was maid-of-honor, and Scott had his best friend from high school stand up with him as best man. We tried to keep the wedding small by inviting just family and a handful of our closest friends. It was truly a beautiful wedding.

I had purchased my wedding gown at a small boutique in Middlebury, Connecticut. Krista and I had spent the day out together having a picnic lunch and looking for the perfect dress. I wanted something elegant, and that would compliment my youthful age. The dress we ended up selecting was a beautiful gown designed by

Jessica McClintock. It was a long sleeve satin gown with a v-neck bodice made of the most gorgeous lace. The gown had a tea length full skirt with a satin bow in the back. Krista thought we had definitely found one of Cinderella's dresses.

We spent five wonderful months together as Mr. and Mrs. Scott Linwood before he was shipped out to Korea for a year-long tour. The first four months of our marriage was spent stationed at Fort Hood in Killeen, Texas. I can't say that I minded spending the winter months in Texas. We didn't have the snow blizzards and harsh below zero weather to deal with.

Killeen was my first experience with living in a military town, and I found it fascinating. Watching the soldiers march in formation while calling cadences to keep in step was exciting to watch. It gave me a sense of pride to know that my husband was a part of the military.

Spending four months in a town wasn't much time to start anything serious, like attending college, and I wanted to spend as much time possible with Scott before he left for Korea. I worked part-time at a Wendy's restaurant right off base while Scott was working, but I always tried to have supper ready when he arrived home from a long and tiresome day.

Our apartment was tiny, about four hundred square feet, but it was our first home together as a married couple, and I thought it was wonderful. It was just off the base next to the Army air field, and I enjoyed hearing the military helicopters coming and going.

I was jogging five to six miles a day now and enjoyed jogging by the air field and watching the enormous helicopters taking off. My favorite military helicopter was the Black Hawk. Scott told me that they were used for a wide array of military missions, including transporting of troops, warfare, and aero medical evacuation. They were powerful pieces of machinery, and the size of the Black Hawks seemed enormous. I was willing to bet that a few of our apartments could fit into one of them. Whenever I saw one taking off or landing, it always boosted my adrenaline and gave me a feeling of pride.

The last month before Scott left for overseas he took a month leave. We decided we'd take our honeymoon in that month and just enjoy life before our long separation. We didn't have a lot of money, but luckily I was able to save a little while being a nanny. It wasn't going to get us a honeymoon in Hawaii, like I dreamed, but at least we were getting the opportunity to spend some alone time together before our separation. We left what little belongings we had in military storage for the year and took what clothes we needed.

Our honeymoon consisted of visiting one of the world's largest underground chamber caves called Carlsbad Caverns in Carlsbad, New Mexico. We stayed two nights in a small motel in the Guadalupe Mountains and visited Carlsbad Caverns one of the days. It was an enormous and very beautiful cave, but I'd have to say the bat flight was the most interesting. At sunset, hundreds of thousands of bats came spilling out from a gigantic hole in the earth, whirling around in a circular motion, and were silhouetted against a vibrant-colored desert sky. It was a beautiful sight to see, especially while curled up in Scott's arms to keep warm on a cool evening.

We also visited Scott's Uncle Lloyd at Grand Lake in Oklahoma. We stayed a week before heading back to Kansas, where I would be living with my parents while he was away.

"Courteney...Courteney, are you about ready to leave for the airport?" asked mom opening my bedroom door.

I had changed my outfit three times trying to figure out what looked best. I was a nervous wreck about Scott seeing me after eight long months of separation. The last time he saw me, I wore size three jeans. Now I was nine months pregnant and had gained eighty pounds in my pregnancy. Even my maternity jeans wouldn't fit over my swollen belly. I figured he might run in the other direction when he saw me.

"I'll be out in a minute. Mom, how does this outfit look? I'm so big, and everything I try on just doesn't look or feel right."

"You look wonderful, Courteney. Scott isn't going to care how big you are. You're carrying his baby. He'll just be happy to see you."

"Thanks, Mom. I guess I'll just settle for this outfit," I replied feeling the baby giving me a swift kick.

"The baby is kicking. Do you want to feel?"

"You know I do," Mom replied with a smile.

My parents were excited about their first grandchild being born. Mom placed her hand on my enlarged belly, but of course the baby decided to stop kicking. I thumped my belly to see if he would kick back. No luck.

"I guess he has a mind of his own," I said laughing. "I hope this isn't a sign of his personality." We both laughed knowing that if this baby boy was strong willed that he got that trait honestly from his mother.

Two weeks had passed since Scott had arrived home from Korea, and our baby boy still hadn't made an appearance. The doctor had decided that they would have to help the baby out a little and would induce labor in the morning.

"Are you nervous about labor, Courteney?" Scott asked attempting to wrap his arms around my enormous belly.

Giving him a warm and enduring hug I replied, "Yes, I guess I am. I hadn't thought much about labor and delivery until recently. Truthfully, I've been trying not to think about it."

"Everything will be okay. I'll be with you the entire time," Scott said giving me a soft kiss and holding me in his arms. How I had missed being held by Scott and having our long talks.

"Scott, what do you want to name our baby boy?"

"What do you have in mind, Courteney?"

"I wanted to name him something different, not a name you hear everyday," I replied hoping he wouldn't disagree with me.

"I know you, Courteney. You already have something in mind. Let me hear it."

"Well, I was thinking about Colby. . . Colby Dale. Dale would be after my father and brother's middle name."

"That is fine. You're the one who has had to carry him nine and a half long months; you should get to name him."

"But do you like the name?"

Taking me into his arms and giving me one of his long, warm kisses he replied, "I love it, just like I love you."

Knowing I had a long day ahead of me, I suggested that we should rest and try to get some sleep. Scott curled up next to me and wrapped his arms around my swollen belly that held our first baby boy.

Drifting off to sleep, Scott whispered, "Relax, Courteney. Everything will be fine. I love you."

"I love you, Scott."

Scott was sound asleep way before me. It felt wonderful to have him lying in bed next to me. I could feel the warmth of his body, and when I put my head on his chest I felt and heard the beating of his heart. Tears started burning my eyes. They slowly made their way down my cheeks. I had so many different emotions consuming me, and being away from Scott had been more difficult than I had imagined.

My father didn't help with making it any easier while Scott was away. His unwise comments he made in the evenings while having his mixed drinks were more than I could handle at times. Many evenings I would call Scott in Korea and talk with him. Sometimes I wouldn't catch him at the barracks and would have to call back later. My father had to voice his opinion at times and let me know that he was probably off with some other girl.

"Men can't go without sex for that long, Courteney. I hope you know that he is probably seeing someone else while he's over there," he'd state while downing another drink. "I'm sure he'll lie about it if you ask him. You'd be a fool to believe him."

His words felt like a slap in the face and ripped at my heart every time I heard them. I wanted to run someplace private and start my bingeing and purging cycle all over again. I didn't dare though for fear of hurting the baby. I wanted to talk to mom about dad's comments, but I knew it wouldn't do any good. Mom always covered up dad's behavior and made excuses for him. We were scolded for not respecting our father and usually told we were lying.

Now that Scott was lying next to me, I never wanted to let go again. I knew in two weeks he'd have to go back to Korea for his last four months of his tour. I wanted to talk with him about the comments my father made, but knew it would infuriate him. What if something happened to Scott like it did to Patrick? I couldn't even think that way; it was too much to endure.

I still thought of Patrick everyday and talked to him when I said my daily prayer. Luckily, my parents' house wasn't far from where he was buried, and I went there often to talk and be close to him. Guilt still consumed me for not being honest with Patrick about my illness. Now I shared my secret with two others, the Lord and Patrick. I hoped Patrick would forgive me for not telling him. There have been many times that I wanted to share my secret with Patrick and Scott, but somehow I would lose my courage.

My eating disorder was better throughout my entire pregnancy. I didn't dare binge, purge, or take any laxatives while I was pregnant. I had told myself that my body belonged to my baby now, and there was no way I was going to do anything to hurt my precious unborn son. Now that I wouldn't be sharing my body with our baby boy anymore, I worried about starting back with my eating disorder. I sure didn't want to fall back into the same cycle that seemed to consume my life before I had gotten pregnant. Even when I was first married to Scott, I managed to binge and purge at least two to three times a week without him noticing.

Curling up closer to Scott, I wiped away my tears. "Lord, I'm feeling so many different emotions right now that I'm not sure where to start. Thank you, Lord, for this wonderful husband you have blessed me with. Help me get through our last four months of separation. I've never been through childbirth before, and I'm scared yet excited about what tomorrow will bring. Help me to be the mother I need to be for our baby boy. Thank you Lord for all my blessings—Amen," I whispered into the silence of the room.

It had been a long day of labor pains then emergency surgery to get our newest member of our small family to enter this world. All of the agonizing pain was soon forgotten when I finally laid eyes on our tiny newborn son. He had finally entered the world at six o'clock in the evening weighing eight pounds twelve ounces and measured twenty-one inches long. Pride swelled up inside of me when I first saw him. I couldn't believe that Scott and I had our first son together.

Scott was cradling his newborn son in one arm while sitting next to me on the hospital bed. I leaned against him and watched our precious little Colby Dale sleeping peacefully in his father's arms.

"He is beautiful, Courteney. You did a wonderful job taking care of him while I was away," Scott said kissing the top of my head.

Tears were starting to roll down my cheeks as I replied, "He is beautiful, isn't he?" I stroked his tiny head feeling the softness of his skin and slightly damp hair. "He has beautiful red hair, and he even smells like a baby," I said with a teasing laugh.

"The nurses bathed him and put baby lotion on him," Scott replied.

Scott and I just watched our baby for the longest time not saying a word to one another. We were mesmerized by this tiny being that was a part of our family now. Colby looked so sweet, one hand clutching the edge of his blue baby blanket and the other curled up into a tiny fist by his cheek.

Stroking his wrist I asked Scott, "What is this on his wrist and hand?" It was red and had a bumpy texture to it; unlike the rest of his skin that was so smooth.

"The doctor said it's a strawberry birthmark. In time it will possibly fade away. Even if it doesn't fade, Courteney, he is still perfect," Scott replied with pride showing on his face.

I reached down and smoothed out his blankets and touched his soft rosy cheek with the back of my hand. Colby was so content in his father's arms. He appeared so tiny lying on his father's chest.

"He is perfect, Scott. I love you so much," I said giving him a kiss.

"You need your rest, Courteney. You've had a long day," he said standing up and tucking the blankets around me. "You get some sleep, and we'll visit with family later. I'm taking Colby back to the nursery."

"Don't take him to the nursery, Scott. Will you place him next to me while I rest?"

"Only if you promise to get some rest," Scott replied giving me a gentle kiss and placing Colby by my side.

"I promise I will." I was feeling tired and knew it would do me good to sleep.

Our precious little Colby was wrapped snuggly in his baby blanket sound asleep. I wrapped my arm around him and whispered, "I love you, Colby Dale."

I just couldn't stop looking at him. He was truly remarkable, and the unconditional love that I was experiencing was an amazing feeling. Stroking his little hand, he stirred and wrapped his five tiny fingers around my big finger and held on tight. I smiled knowing that I was truly going to enjoy being a mother.

"Lord, thank you for this precious child. He is perfect. Help me to be the mother I need to be for Colby," I spoke softly as I drifted off to sleep.

Summer of 1989, My Decision

Rolling over onto my side, I stared at Scott while he was still sleeping peacefully. Adjusting the pillow to a more comfortable position, I started thinking back over the last year and a half of Scott and I being married. So much had changed for both of us.

Most of our marriage had been spent apart, and now that we were finally together again, we were parents. The last four months of his tour in Korea had gone by faster than I thought it would. The baby kept me busy which helped with the loneliness I felt while Scott was serving time overseas.

Colby was growing faster than a weed, and everyday seemed like a blessing to have him in our lives. I loved to hear him laugh and watch him kick and wave his arms in excitement. He was a healthy baby and only had to go to the doctor for his regular checkups. God had blessed us with a wonderful, healthy son, and I was thankful for this blessing.

Colby received a lot of attention from strangers with his red hair and multi-colored eyes. His left eye was a baby blue color like mine, and the right eye was blue and brown striped. His eyes were unique and he truly was an adorable baby.

We both loved being parents, but the financial strain was something we hadn't given much thought to before stepping into parenthood. To help make ends meet I was working part-time as a waitress at Red Lobster just off base. I tried to adjust my work schedule so it didn't overlap with Scott's. This way we didn't have an added expense of daycare.

Scott had been stationed at Fort Sill in Lawton, Oklahoma. Ft. Sill is home of the field artillery. Scott was going to be attending Advanced Individual Training here. As far as I could tell, he enjoyed his work.

I could hear Colby stirring in his bed and knew he would want to be eating soon. Leaning on my elbow, I leaned over and kissed Scott softly so I wouldn't wake him then quietly slipped out of bed. It was still early in the morning. I knew Scott would sleep in late. He wasn't an early morning person.

Picking up the baby I quietly spoke, "Good morning, little one. How are you this morning?"

Giving him a kiss and hug I asked, "Are you ready to eat, little one?"

I changed his diaper and sat down in the rocking chair to nurse him. The nurses at the hospital had asked me if I was going to nurse my baby. In the beginning I wasn't sure, but I am glad that I decided to. The nurses had informed me that a mother's milk is healthier for the baby and it also builds a bond between mother and baby. They were right. It is an amazing feeling to know that I have the ability to sustain and nourish my baby with the milk that my body produces.

Unfortunately, I wasn't sure how much longer I would be able to nurse Colby. My milk seemed to be drying up and it was getting harder to nurse him with working in the evenings. Eventually the day would come when I would have to stop nursing. I dreaded that day not only because it was my special alone time with Colby, but I was afraid what it meant for me.

I hadn't binged or purged since I had been pregnant or nursing the baby. The desire was still there and very strong. Once I stopped nursing, I knew there was nothing to stop me from returning to my old eating habits.

I could hear Scott stirring around in the bedroom. Something was very different about Scott since he had arrived home from Korea. There was harshness in the way he spoke to me, and I wasn't feeling the closeness that I once felt with him. How to make things better was a puzzle to me.

Why had our relationship taken a turn for the worse? The financial strain we were experiencing or perhaps he had been with another girl in Korea had crossed my mind. There were times when

I didn't handle the stress in our household well, and would stay out late with friends after I got off work. I knew my actions weren't going to help the situation, but I was at a loss and felt stressed and anxious most of the time.

Scott walked out of the bedroom and into the kitchen without saying a word. This was routine for him lately. Sometimes it would take thirty minutes to an hour before he would say a word.

I thought I'd try to break the ice by saying, "Good morning Scott."

"Hey," he said with a gruff voice.

"Did you sleep well?" I asked trying to make conversation.

"I'm still tired. I just needed something to drink. What time do you work tonight?"

"I work five to close tonight," I said lifting the baby onto my shoulder.

"When is your mother coming in to stay for the summer?" asked Scott.

"She'll be coming in a week from tomorrow," I replied.

He went outside to smoke a cigarette and went back to bed. He spoke not another word to me that day.

Before we got married, I use to think about what it would be like to be married to Scott. I had mapped everything out carefully, thinking we'd be the perfect couple. Even when we would get into disagreements, they wouldn't last long, and we'd have enjoyable ways of making up. The closeness I felt with him would never disappear, even through marital spats. My life felt like it was crumbling, and I didn't know how to put it back together. I didn't even understand why it was all falling apart. How was I to fix something when I wasn't sure of what to fix?

I had talked with my mother over the phone many times about the situation. She was concerned and wanted to come for the summer to help out with the baby. I knew her intentions were good, but I wasn't so sure if having another person in the household would make the situation better or just add more stress. Time would tell. She would be here next week, and I was looking forward to having some much needed help.

"Is this where you work?" my mother asked while driving back to our apartment from picking her up at the airport.

"Yes, and Ft. Sill is right here," I said pointing in the direction of the base. "The military base brings a lot of customers into the restaurant."

"Maybe Scott will give you a tour of the base while you are here."

"That would be great," mom replied.

"I appreciate you coming to help with Colby," I said gently touching my mother's arm.

Giving me one of her welcoming warm smiles she replied, "You're welcome, Courteney. I'm just thankful I have the summer off to be able to do things like this. I can't think of a better way to spend my summer than helping out with my first born grandson."

We pulled into our driveway. Leaning over to give her a hug I replied, "Thanks again for everything."

"Hi, Mom," Scott said cheerfully while opening the car door. "Let me help you two gals get bags carried into the house."

"That would be great," I replied tiredly.

"I'll get the baby," Mom stated with enthusiasm in her voice. "I've been waiting to get my hands on this little one ever since I arrived at the airport," she said picking him up and giving him a smothering grandma hug and kiss.

Colby didn't seem to mind and squealed with delight. He just loved being held and getting special attention from his grandma.

We did very little the rest of the day. Mom took Colby for a long walk while I managed to throw together a quick dinner. We ate in the front room while watching a movie on television. As tired as I felt, I knew I wouldn't make it through the entire movie without falling asleep.

"Courteney... Courteney, wake up. Go on to bed, Courteney. I'll feed the baby a bottle and put him down for the night," Mom said shaking my shoulder to get my attention.

I wasn't going to argue as tired as I was.

"Thanks, Mom," I said sleepily.

"Goodnight, little one," I said, giving Colby a soft kiss on the left cheek.

"Night, Scott. Are you coming to bed?"

"Not until the movie is over. Goodnight, Courteney."

When I turned to head back to the bedroom I suddenly felt light-headed and everything started turning black. I put my hand on the wall to keep from falling.

"Are you all right, Courteney," Scott and Mom said simultaneously.

"I'm fine. I'm just tired. See you in the morning."

I slipped into my pajamas and curled up underneath the warm quilt my grandmother had made. One good thing about our apartment was the air conditioner worked great. Oklahoma was just like Kansas in the summer, hot and muggy. Scott and I kept the apartment cool so we'd sleep better.

Reaching over to the night stand, I turned on the radio. I started thinking about what tomorrow would bring.

I had to work in the evening, but I would do my daily workout before heading to work. I had joined the gym in town and was working out one to two hours a day. Usually, I jogged on the track for an hour and then attended an hour aerobics class. I've acquired the nickname of energizer bunny at the gym. Sometimes I wonder myself where I do manage to get my energy.

There was a nursery at the gym where Colby stayed while I did my workout. One of the teenage girls that worked there just loved Colby. She spoiled him by holding him the entire time. Their favorite game to play was peek-a-boo.

I had stopped nursing Colby. Unfortunately, I was struggling with my eating disorder again. I had feared I would return to the same old pattern of bingeing, purging, taking laxatives, and then fasting for a two to three day period. It was easy vomiting after every meal without anyone suspecting. All I had to do was turn on the water in the bathroom, which always drowned out the sound of induced vomiting. Scott and my mother never suspected anything.

The bulimia and excessive exercising had a tendency to make me feel tired. Every opportunity I could get, I tried to sleep.

There was a part of me that hated my eating habits, and I wanted to stop. It had become a part of me though, and I feared letting go.

My life seemed messed up in so many ways. I wasn't feeling close to my husband anymore, I was disappointing my parents because I wasn't going to college, and I truthfully just didn't know what I wanted out of life.

I could feel the tears burning my eyes and threatening to fall uncontrollably. Crying myself to sleep was becoming a ritual.

"Lord, why do I feel so empty and sad inside? Why do I cry so easily? Why does my life seem so messed up?" I whispered softly as I drifted off to sleep.

I didn't have the answers. More than anything I wished somebody could help me find the answers to these questions.

The summer flew by quickly, and mom would be going back to Kansas soon. It was great having extra help around the house. Mom helped take care of the baby, cleaned, and fixed meals. It was truly a blessing to have extra help.

The tension between Scott and I was unfortunately not any better. He seemed angry at Colby and me a lot. If I tried to talk with him about why he spoke so hateful and short towards me, he just shut me out. It was like he had built a wall around himself, and he shared his thoughts with no one. I felt totally alienated from our once affectionate marriage.

Reaching for our wedding picture, the tears started burning my cheeks. This wedding photo was one of my favorites. We were dancing our first dance together as a married couple. The love and passion I felt in that picture was what I desired to feel again. How I wished I could feel the closeness we felt when we were first married.

"Are you all right, Courteney?" Mom asked startling me.

"I'm sorry. I thought I was alone," I replied wiping away the tears with the back of my hand.

"What's the matter?" Mom asked sitting next to me on the couch.

"I don't know, Mom. Everything just seems wrong. I can't talk with Scott anymore. Our relationship seems to be falling apart, and I don't know what to do to make it better," I said crying uncontrollably.

Mom put her arms around me and let me cry until I couldn't cry anymore.

"Courteney, you know I like Scott, but you two are different. You were raised in different kinds of households with different values. We talked about this before, and I know you just didn't see it then. Maybe you can see now how difficult it is for two people from different worlds to come together and survive as a married couple."

"It is true that we are opposites, but that is one of the qualities that attracted me to Scott," I said sniffling. "There is something different about Scott and our relationship since he returned from overseas. Maybe it is me. I just don't know," I retorted standing up hastily to put some space between my mother and I.

"Why are you getting upset with me, Courteney? I have done nothing but help out all summer and then you get snippy with me," Mom snapped back.

"You're right, Mom. I'm sorry for snapping at you. I do appreciate everything you have done for Scott and me. You have helped so much this summer, and Colby has enjoyed having you around. I'm just frustrated, and I feel like I'm losing my husband. My life is falling apart. I don't know how to put it back together," I replied sitting back down next to her and crying softly.

I wanted to tell her everything about my eating disorder. I wanted to let her know I had been bingeing and purging two to three times a day, taking huge amounts of laxatives, and then starving myself for three days while exercising excessively. No one even noticed that my knuckles had cuts and sores on them, or the fact that I always had a sore throat. It hurt to swallow when I did eat, and I was constantly having stomach cramps. Why didn't anyone even notice?

For years I had been telling myself that I could stop when I was ready. I was lying to myself and everyone that I loved. My life was becoming a mound of lies to cover up my behavior that I didn't want discovered. This illness was highly addictive and more powerful than I ever imagined it could be. I never meant for it to get this out of control and to hurt everyone I loved.

"A penny for your thoughts, Courteney. You want to share what you're thinking," she said putting her arm around my trembling shoulders.

Looking her in the eyes I knew I couldn't tell her. I replied, "No, Mom, I'm just numb and I feel lost. I love Scott and don't want to lose him. If I lose him, what do I have?"

"You have your son, Courteney," Mom replied.

"I know that. I am blessed to have such a wonderful little boy. He definitely keeps me going from day to day. My life would seem pretty empty without him."

"What about school, Courteney? Don't you want to go back to school and get an education? That is important if you want to support yourself and a child on your own," Mom stated.

"I'm not on my own, Mom. Even though there are problems between Scott and me, we are still together. School is important to me, and I will go back when I am ready."

"Like I said, Courteney, I do like Scott. I do think you need to reconsider being married to him though. His family has never made education a priority, or had high goals for themselves in life. You will fall into the same trap married to him," she stated. "Look at Scott's father and how he has abandoned his wife and children so many times. You see how he just picked up and left his wife for another woman after over twenty years of marriage. Scott is a lot like his father, and it is only a matter of time before he does the same to you. What do you have then, Courteney? How will you support yourself? Is that the life you want?" Mom stated with a firm tone to her voice.

Mom waited for an answer to all her explicit questions.

Leaning back against the couch in complete exhaustion and feeling like this was a no win situation, I finally answered.

"Of course I do not want my life to end like that, mother. How am I supposed to support a baby on my own? The expense is far greater than I expected, and I don't have a dime to my name. What will I do with Colby while I'm at school? How will I pay for school?"

Mom replied, "You can live with your father and me. There is plenty of room at the house. You can get student loans to pay for your education and we will help with Colby. Please, Courteney, think about this. It is what is best for you and the baby."

"I can't leave with you now, but I will think about what you've said. If things don't get better with Scott, then I promise I will move back home. Just give me time to think things through," I stated crying softly.

"I know things seem difficult now, Courteney, but in the long run you will be better off with someone more like you. You are an intelligent and beautiful young lady that needs to get an education and find a gentleman that has an education too. You will find that life will be easier with someone more like yourself," stated Mom.

"All I can say is that I promise to think about everything you've said. I'm getting tired and my stomach is hurting. I think I'll lie down for a while," I said giving her a hug and dismissing myself to my bedroom.

Turning on the radio, I laid down on the bed to rest. Wrapping the warm blanket around my trembling body, I started to go over in my mind everything mom believed. Was mom correct about Scott and me? Crying softly, I realized that there may be some truth to her words.

Four months passed and our relationship had grown worse, along with my eating disorder. Two weeks after Colby's first birthday, I told Scott the dreadful news. I was leaving him and heading home to Kansas with Colby. This is not what I had planned or wanted for myself or Colby. The last thing I wanted to do was take his father away from him.

I dreamed of the loving and affectionate relationship we once had, having many children with Scott and growing old together. I needed to stop dreaming and face reality. Reality was our relationship had grown distant and cold. I often wondered if this was God's way of punishing me for all the lies I told to cover up my secret.

By the spring semester of 1990, I was enrolled full-time at Kansas City Kansas Community College in Kansas City, Kansas, and had filed for a divorce. The day I actually left Scott was worse than I had imagined. My heart still felt like it had been ripped and was permanently broken.

The day regrettably came that our divorce was final. When we had to appear in court, I lost my nerve and didn't think I could go through with it. How could I lose Scott forever? He was my life, my soul mate. My mother reassured me of her beliefs and told me I could do this. That life would get better. I wasn't so sure about anything getting better.

The pain and sorrow I was feeling the day of our divorce was more than I could handle. It's weird how your mind will bury painful experiences and make you feel numb.

I turned to my eating disorder to try to induce some peace and happiness into my life. My eating disorder helped mask my feelings of sorrow and being a failure.

Scott informed me that he was being sent to Germany shortly after our divorce. I didn't know when I would see him again. How would Colby ever get to know his father and spend the quality time that a boy needed with his father? This was my fault, and I needed to do something to set things right.

No one still knew anything about me being bulimic. All the lies I had to tell to cover up my illness had damaged my relationship with Scott. How could I have let this happen? I knew what I had to do to make things better. I had to tell Scott the truth about my illness. Maybe he would understand and would forgive me for all the pain it has caused between us. The hate that showed in his eyes when he looked at me broke my heart.

A few days before he left for Germany, I finally got up the nerve to call him. I asked him if I could come over and talk with him. He was reluctant at first, but I insisted it was important.

As I was pulling into his parents' driveway my body was trembling so hard that I didn't think I'd be able to walk to the door. Taking a deep breath to calm myself, I stepped out of the car and headed to the house. There was no backing down; I had to tell him about my illness. I needed help.

Knocking on the door I heard a voice behind me say, "Hi, Courteney."

I turned around to see Scott standing at the side of the house.

"Hi, Scott," I said with a trembling voice.

"Are you all right? You don't look so good," he said stepping towards me.

"We need to talk, Scott. Where is Colby?"

"My sister took him for a walk so we could talk," he replied. Scott was spending time with Colby before he left for Germany. He wasn't sure when he would be back again to see him.

Scott opened the door and stepped into the house saying, "Let's talk inside."

Following him into the house I asked, "Is anyone else home?"

"No, we're alone. What do you want to say?"

I sat down in the nearest chair and stared at the floor for the longest time. I couldn't find the right words.

"Are you going to say anything, Courteney, or are you just going to sit there and stare at the floor?" he asked with agitation in his voice.

I didn't blame him for being angry with me. I had stripped him of his family and he was experiencing all the pain I was feeling. I didn't wish that pain even on my worst enemy. The tension between us was making it hard to find the words I wanted to say.

"I need to tell you something, Scott, that may come as a shock to you. I don't even know why I'm telling you. Maybe this is a mistake," I said standing up heading towards the door.

"Come and sit down, Courteney. I'm listening. You have me curious now. I want to hear what you have to say," he stated.

Sitting back down in the chair and crying uncontrollably, the words finally came out. "I have an eating disorder. I have had it for many years, and I am scared because it has gotten out of control. I don't know how to stop." Pausing for a minute to catch my breath I went on, "I'm scared I'm going to die from this illness. I never meant for it to get out of control."

There was a long period of silence from Scott. I'm sure he couldn't believe what he had heard. I sat there crying and shaking uncontrollably.

Getting up from the couch he came over and put his arms around me and said, "Everything is going to be all right, Courteney."

He held me in his arms and let me cry for the longest time. It felt wonderful to be in his arms. I almost forgot we were actually divorced. Then I remembered we weren't husband and wife anymore and pulled back quickly.

"I'm sorry, Scott. I probably shouldn't have told you about my eating disorder, but I felt I had to before you left for Germany," I stated shivering slightly.

"I'm glad you told me, Courteney. We need to get you better so you are able to take care of and be there for our son," he replied firmly.

Staring at me in silence for the longest time he finally said, "We need to tell your parents, Courteney. I won't be here to help you. I have orders to go to Germany."

"No, Scott. I can't tell them. My father wouldn't want to hear about it anyway. You know him well enough to know that he doesn't talk about anything negative. It will just hurt my mother, and she will never understand," I blurted out.

"Courteney, we have to tell them. We will just sit down with your mother and tell her. She would want to know. I'm sorry I can't be here for you, but I don't have a choice. I have to go to Germany."

Putting my face down into my hands, I thought about what Scott said. Disappearing off the face of earth would be a lot easier than having to tell my parents I had an eating disorder.

"Courteney, what eating disorder do you have?"

"I am bulimic," I stated feeling a shiver go through my body.

Scott wasn't familiar with eating disorders. We spent sometime talking about my eating habits. I didn't tell him everything, but I told him enough to familiarize him with my behaviors. It wasn't easy for me to talk about.

We decided that he would come to my house tonight to talk to my mother together. We agreed to let her tell dad her own way. The idea of telling my mother made my stomach turn. This is not what I had hoped for. I had hoped that Scott would take me with him and help me recover from this illness without my parents knowing. Maybe that would still happen. Time would tell.

Scott did all the talking to my mother. I couldn't speak a word, but the tears were falling steadfast. He told her all I had told him. He wanted a promise from her that I would get the help I needed while he was gone.

"Of course we will help her, Scott," Mom said sympathetically. "Thank you for telling us before you left overseas."

Mom came over and gently put her arms around me.

"Why didn't you tell us, Courteney? Everything is going to be all right," she softly whispered trying to hold back the tears.

I knew she was trying to be strong for me, but eventually we both gave in and cried.

"Courteney, I do need to get going. I have a lot of packing to do before I leave tomorrow," Scott stated.

I could feel my heart sinking into the pit of my stomach. How I wanted to throw my arms around Scott and never let him go. I didn't know when I would see him again, or if I would ever again. What if something happened to him while he was gone? Three years was a long time. He could possibly meet someone else and remarry in that amount of time. Since we did have a son together, I would probably see him again sometime, but what if he was remarried. The thought of him with somebody else tore at my heart.

"Will you write to us, Scott?" I asked wiping the tears off my cheeks with the back of my hand.

"You know I'm not the best at writing, but I'll do my best. I will drop Colby off at your work tomorrow on my way to the airport," he said speaking to my mother.

"That will be fine," she replied.

Giving me a hug, Scott said, "Get better, Courteney. Not only for yourself, but for our son that needs you. He loves you and needs you in his life, Courteney." Trying to hold back the tears, but failing miserably, he spoke his last words before he left.

"Write to me, Courteney, and let me know how you are. You are a strong person and can beat this illness. I do care about you. Goodbye," he said pulling away from me and heading out the door.

Watching him pull out of the driveway was difficult. Would I ever see him again? I wish I knew the answer.

Exhausted and filled with pain, I climbed the stairs to the bedroom I would be occupying while living with my parents. I didn't even bother to eat or speak to my parents the rest of the evening. I wanted to be left alone. I had lost all of my dreams of building a life with Scott and growing old together. What I was feeling now was exactly how I felt when I found out that Patrick had passed away.

How would I make it without Scott? How was I ever going to stop being bulimic? I didn't have the answers.

"Lord, I'm beginning to wonder if you hear my prayers. Please help me Lord. I don't know if I can make it another day with all this sorrow I feel."

The Meeting

A year had passed since Scott had left for Germany, but regrettably, I cannot say things were better. My eating disorder was still a major problem in my life, and I hadn't heard a word from Scott. I took that as a message that he didn't want anything ever to do with me again. I blamed my eating disorder. Who would want to be married to someone who was so sick with so many problems?

My parents reminded me often how they were correct about him. "I told you, Courteney, he would eventually abandon you and your son. You won't ever see him again. Move on with your life, Courteney," they said so often without even considering how it made me feel.

My secret was known now by my parents, but hardly a word was ever spoken about it. Once in a while my mother would ask me how I was, or what I was doing to make things better.

The first time I went to the counseling center to get information about eating disorders, my mother was attempting to be supportive and read the pamphlet. She was defensive and upset by what she had read.

This is what it said:

> There are a number of factors that contribute to the development of eating disorders. Some factors that contribute to eating disorders are biological, genetic, cultural, or a direct result from the family environment in which the individual is raised. When parents set unrealistically high expectations on a child, the child

can develop an eating disorder to cope with feelings of inadequacy and as a way to control at least one area of their life. Children receive their first messages about their bodies from parents. If there is too much of an emphasis on physical appearance, the child can develop a low self-esteem.

When my mother read this information, she didn't even bother reading the rest of the pamphlet. She immediately became defensive and made the statement, "Oh, so this is supposedly our fault. Well no one is going to blame your illness on us. We have done nothing wrong."

I tried to tell her that no one was blaming them. She didn't believe me and stayed defensive. I have never blamed anyone, but myself, for my eating disorder. I hated this illness called bulimia nervosa. I hated the shame and defensiveness it spread through our home. I hated the sadness and hopelessness I felt all the time. I know God says that you are not to hate, but I was determined to hate this illness forever.

My sister, Kelli, was trying her hardest to be supportive. She often told me that she was at a loss of what to do for me, but reminded me how much she loved me and wanted me to get better.

I'll never forget the night when I collapsed to the ground due to severe stomach pains. I was crying and shaking uncontrollably. Kelli had helped me to the bedroom. She went to our father and told him I needed help. My father was having his usual mixed drinks. When he came into the bedroom his words I will never forget.

"What is it now, Courteney? This is so stupid. Just stop this ridiculous behavior," he said slurring his words together.

Looking at him with anger raging inside of me I hollered, "You just stop your drinking."

My comment didn't go over well. I was told I was being disrespectful; I could just get out of his house.

What saddened me the most was the fact that my father thought everything I stood for was stupid, and my mother was more worried about being blamed for my illness. More than anything, I wanted them to worry about helping me get better and not worry about who is to blame. What good was it going to do to go around blaming others? Truthfully, I was more worried about dying from this illness and leaving my son without his mother.

Walking into the local guidance center to get information about eating disorders was difficult, but I hadn't taken that step I needed to take. To get better I knew I needed to start talking with a counselor. How I felt about myself, the pain I was experiencing, well I just didn't know if I could talk about it freely with a stranger. I would be opening myself up for criticism that I didn't think I could handle. I knew I was doing wrong; I didn't need to hear more about how stupid my actions were.

My time at Kansas City Kansas Community College was coming to an end, and I needed to start thinking where I wanted to enroll to finish my education degree. I had decided that I would follow in my mother's footsteps and become a teacher. Amazingly, my grades were pretty good. It wasn't going to be a problem getting into another school. I decided to enroll at Missouri Western State College in St. Joseph, Missouri. My life changed considerably while attending Missouri Western.

It was the fall of 1991; the trees were changing into their beautiful autumn colors just like my life took on an enormous change. I had moved out of my parents' home and was renting an apartment in St. Joseph, Missouri. When I first started attending school there, things were basically the same. I was having problems with my eating disorder, exercising excessively, and doing my best to keep up with school and raising my little boy.

Colby kept the desire to fight this illness within me. There were weeks when I did fairly well in controlling my illness, but there were days when I failed miserably. I had failed a lot of people that I loved. I was determined not to fail my son and leave him without a mother.

Prayer was a daily ritual, but I didn't dare step foot inside a church. There was so much I didn't understand about religion. I was ashamed of this and didn't want others knowing. My deep down gut feeling was that if I wanted to get better, I needed God in my life. So I prayed, but in the privacy of my own home.

One day while on campus, I was walking down the hallway to my next class. A guy accidentally slammed into me and my books went flying. He apologized and helped with picking up my things. As he was walking off, I noticed a flyer on the bulletin board on the wall. It was advertising an informational meeting about eating disorders. I knew this was a meeting I needed to attend. I wrote down the date and time, and promised myself that I would go.

When I attended the meeting, I received a small booklet filled with information about eating disorders. The people who attended the meeting were girls. In the beginning we stated that we were there to get information for a school report, not because we were suffering from an eating disorder. By the end of the meeting, there were tears flowing and general confessions being made.

This meeting made a difference in my life. Not once had I ever thought about others that may be suffering with the same illness. I wasn't alone in this battle. This room was filled with girls just like me. They were beautiful girls from all American families just like mine. Yet, they were suffering immensely inside and didn't know how to make life better.

I recognized one of the women who organized this informational meeting. She was a teacher on campus that taught some of the physical education classes. She was a young woman, I'd say in her young thirties, with a pleasant personality. She had always greeted me with a smile and a hello in the hallways. Her name was Mrs. Kelly.

When Mrs. Kelly spoke, everyone seemed to be listening carefully. She was one of those people that you were drawn to and felt you could trust.

This is what she said:

> Ladies, I want to thank you for coming here tonight. If you are here because you feel you are suffering from an eating disorder, then you have taken a huge step. A

step that is difficult, but an important step that can make a difference in your life. I won't lie to you. Recovering from an eating disorder is a long process and is extremely difficult. The sickness you are suffering from is far easier to deal with than admitting to yourself you are ill and going through the steps needed to recover. It is an exhausting fight, and you will want to give up at times. You will feel like you're on an emotional roller coaster. I am here tonight to let you know that it is a fight worth fighting, no matter how difficult it may be. Our school nurse is here to inform you of the programs available in starting this courageous journey.

I couldn't imagine the process of recovery being any harder than suffering from this illness. Her words were permanently embedded in my mind, and I was terrified at the thought of the pain and suffering getting worse. Was I willing to fight for my life? I knew the answer to this question. I was willing to fight. Not only to insure that my son would have a mother, but for myself. My desire to live was far greater than my desire for death.

The school nurse went on to explain more about recovery. This is what she said:

Mrs. Kelly is correct about the extreme difficulty that goes along with fighting an eating disorder. Every person is unique, and what works for one individual may be ineffective for another. It takes months, even years to recover.

It is important that the eating disorder sufferer be ready for treatment and believes in what they are fighting for. With an eating disorder, you are fighting for your life. There are many who die from this illness.

An individual must be willing to commit themselves to the eating disorder program that is set up for them. There are inpatient and outpatient programs available. You will receive different forms of counseling including nutrition, individual, group, and family. The longer a person has suffered with an eating disorder, the harder it is to treat. Understand that it is not impossible.

Treatment and recovery will seem overwhelming to most eating disorder sufferers. It is a huge commitment that can be frightening and overpowering. I have found in life that when a goal seems overwhelming, it helps to break it down into smaller goals that will ultimately help you obtain your larger goal. I don't want any of you leaving tonight feeling overwhelmed. I want you to feel proud of yourselves for taking an important step in coming tonight. Most importantly I want you to set a small goal for yourself. Your goal is to make an appointment with me in my office, and let's talk.

When I went home that evening, I was feeling hopeful and scared all at one time. I did what the nurse said and had already accomplished my first goal. I made an appointment to visit with her tomorrow morning.

I wondered how many little goals I was going to have to set for myself to reach my ultimate goal. She had stated that the longer you had an eating disorder, the harder it is to recover. I had been bulimic for almost ten years now. Truthfully, I didn't know if that was considered a short or long period of time. How difficult was this fight going to be?

When I tucked Colby in for bed that evening he said to me, "I love you mom." With tears starting to stream down my cheeks I stated, "I love you too sweetheart."

Sitting there for the longest time, I watched him slip into a peaceful sleep.

Curling up next to my little boy, I started to pray, "Lord, thank you for bringing this meeting to my attention. I have so far to travel in my treatment, and so much to learn. I'm scared Lord. I am listening, and I promise I will work hard to get better. Help me to be the mother I need to be for this precious little boy you have blessed me with."

Smiling at my sleeping little boy, I thought about the words he says so often, "I love you mom." Those words reassured me that this fight was well worth fighting.

Nurse Nikki

I was awakened in the early hours of the morning by an energetic little red headed boy giving me a bear hug and a kiss.

"Hi, Mom. Are you awake, Mom?" Colby said with renewed energy.

"Hi, sweetie. I'm awake now," I said returning his kiss and hug.

"Do I get to go to school with you today?" he stated excitedly. Colby loved going to the daycare on campus. Sometimes he would even tell people that he went to college.

He'd always get a cute response like, "You do? I bet the college girls just love you. How old are you?"

"I'm two and a half," he would state proudly.

He did get a lot of attention from the girls on campus. He shied away from most of them. He was extremely bashful towards strangers, but once he got to know you, he would talk your head off.

"Yes, you are going to school with me today, sweetie. In fact we need to get moving. I have an appointment this morning," I said feeling my stomach doing flip flops.

Suddenly, I remembered I had an appointment with the school nurse. I had no idea what to expect, or what questions they might expect me to answer. My entire body started to tremble at the thought of having to walk in there. I took a deep breath to calm myself down. There was no doubt in my mind that I needed to do this, and I was determined to keep my appointment even if my insides felt like they had thousands of butterflies fluttering around.

111

Picking Colby up into my arms I said, "Let's get going, sweetie. We need to get cleaned up, feed you breakfast, and get out the door." I knew I needed to get moving. If I lay there too long and thought about this appointment, I might just change my mind.

Walking into the nurse's office, I glanced at the clock on the wall to see how much time I had before my appointment. I always made a point of being early to appointments, and this one was no exception. It showed that I was about ten minutes early.

Walking up to the desk, I saw the nurse from yesterday's meeting working on some paperwork. She was a young lady, maybe late twenties, with the prettiest long blonde hair. When she spoke at the meeting, her tone of voice gave me the impression that she was pleasant and a trustworthy person.

"Hi. I'm here for an eight o'clock appointment," I stated with a quiver to my voice. I could feel my insides starting to tremble again. How I hated that feeling.

"Hi, Courteney. I'm so glad that you came in this morning. I was looking forward to visiting with you," she stated with a cheerful tone.

"Just call me Nurse Nikki. Why don't you come back to this room and make yourself comfortable," she said leading me to a small room.

The room had a warm and inviting feeling to it. The walls were painted a warm blue color with a pretty flower border. The floor had a large throw rug that matched the flower border. Two plush chairs with a coffee table in between them sat on top of the rug. It wasn't anything like I expected. I guess I was expecting a typical doctor's office with the examining table and a sink.

"Make yourself comfortable, Courteney. Would you like something to drink?"

"No... no thank you," I said sitting down in the nearest chair. I was afraid if I tried to drink anything, it might come right back up.

"Are you cold, Courteney, you're shivering? I could get you a blanket."

"I'll be fine. I'm just a little nervous."

Shutting the door and sitting down into the other chair she stated, "Well, don't be nervous, Courteney. Why don't we start off by you telling me a little bit about yourself. Tell me about some of the things you like to do, your hobbies, what you are majoring in."

Taking a deep breath I started telling her a little about myself.

"I am from Leavenworth, Kansas. I moved to St. Joseph, Missouri, with my two-year-old son to attend Missouri Western. I am majoring in elementary education." Pausing for a minute to get control of my shaking I continued on, "I like to bake with my son, read books, listen to music, and exercise."

"What do you like to bake with your son?"

"We enjoy baking honey cookies. He likes cutting the cookies out into different shapes with the cookie cutters."

"What is your son's name?"

"Colby...Colby Linwood," I stated glancing at the piece of paper she was writing on.

"I'm just writing down information you tell me so I don't forget anything. Is that ok?" she asked sincerely. "I don't want to make you feel uncomfortable."

"No, that is fine. This is just all new to me," I stated trying to relax.

"Well, you're doing great, Courteney. Do you like Missouri Western and the education department?"

"Yes, I do. Everyone is helpful and very kind. I have enjoyed being here. I like the daycare they have on campus. It allows my son to be closer to me while I'm attending classes."

"I'm glad you are having a positive experience here at Missouri Western. I need to ask you some questions now. Some of them may be personal, and if you need time to answer them that is all right," she said smiling at me while flipping her piece of paper over.

"I know your first name is Courteney, but what is your last?"

"My full name is Courteney Baker."

"You attended the eating disorder meeting for what reason?"

Feeling a chill go down my spine I answered, "I am bulimic."

"What are some of your eating behaviors that make you feel you are bulimic?"

Staring at the floor, I was having doubts if I could go on further. Feeling the tears starting to roll down my cheeks, I scolded myself for falling apart in front of a total stranger.

"It's all right, Courteney," she said sincerely. "Let me get you a blanket to keep you warmer," she stated leaving the room. When she returned she had a warm blanket and a glass of water.

I wrapped the blanket around my quivering shoulders, and then drank a small sip of water. I still had doubts if I could keep even a sip down the way my stomach felt.

Putting the glass down on the coffee table I stated, "Thank you. I'm sorry for being so emotional. I cry easily, and this is a difficult subject for me to talk about."

"No need for apologies, Courteney. When you think you are ready, you let me know," she stated with kindness and understanding.

Reaching for a tissue, I wiped my eyes and nose and asked, "Can you repeat the question?"

"Of course. What are some of your eating behaviors that make you feel you are bulimic?"

Without looking at her, I answered her question.

"I binge and purge two to four times a day, take twenty to thirty laxatives afterwards, and then starve myself for two to three days. When I starve myself, I exercise excessively."

"What do you do after you've starved yourself for two or three days?"

"The cycle starts all over again," I said feeling shame and embarrassed by my behavior.

"Have you experienced any medical or physical problems since you have been bulimic? For example, missing your menstrual cycle, stomach problems, chest pains, or problems with your teeth?"

"My periods aren't regular. Sometimes I have stomach cramps that are so severe that I can't walk. About a month ago my back tooth cracked and part of it fell off. I suck on a lot of cough drops, because my throat is always sore," I said pausing for a moment to think if there were any other symptoms. Showing her my right hand I stated, "I also have some cuts and sores on my knuckles."

She took my hand and studied it carefully. "Do you know what those are from?"

"No...I don't."

"That is called Russell's sign. It is caused by repeatedly sticking your fingers down your throat to induce vomiting," she said releasing my hand.

"How old were you when you started being bulimic?"

"I was fourteen years old," I replied finally getting the nerve up to look at her. She was giving me one of her warm smiles.

"How old are you now, Courteney?

"I am twenty-three."

"So it has been about nine to ten years that you have been bulimic?"

"Yes, but I didn't do anything throughout my pregnancy or while nursing my baby. But, I did immediately start back up after I stopped nursing."

"Does anyone else know that you are bulimic?"

"Yes... my ex-husband, my parents, and my sister. I don't know if they have told anyone else."

"You haven't spoken with any other counselor about being bulimic?"

"No...this is the first I've talked with any medical professionals."

"Are you willing to go to an inpatient program if needed?"

"No."

"Why not?"

"I have a little boy. I don't want to leave him."

"Do you have medical insurance?"

"No...I don't. Money could be a problem. I don't have a lot of money being a single mom," I said feeling a little embarrassed by my situation.

"Let's not worry about the money issue. Where there's a will, there's a way. Have you ever heard that expression?"

"Yes, I have."

"Do you understand what it means?"

"Yes, it means that if you set your mind to something, regardless of any handicap that may stand in your way, with determination you can accomplish whatever you want."

"Very good, Courteney. When it comes to your eating disorder, do you feel you are ready to undertake the tough journey you are about to endure? You have been bulimic for quite some time, and it will be tough, but not impossible. You're going to have to be strong and willing to open up to those who want to help you," she stated.

Putting my head down and starting to cry once again, I thought about her question. Am I ready to undertake this tough journey? Am I willing to open up to total strangers?

I started thinking about holding my little boy in my arms, his arms wrapped around my neck, and the words he so often spoke, "I love you, Mom." I thought about Patrick, our love we shared, and the words he so often spoke, "I love you, Courteney." Even Scott's words, "You are a strong person and can beat this illness, Courteney. I do care about you." All of these words started twirling around in my head, and I knew what the answer was.

Lifting my head with tears flowing I said, "Yes, I am ready."

Nurse Nikki stood and walked over to where I was sitting. Patting my back softly and handing me the tissue box she stated, "Everything is going to be all right, Courteney."

She stood there softly patting my back and letting me cry. When the crying lessened, and I could speak again without getting upset I asked, "What do I do now?"

Sitting back down in her chair she responded, "I know a counselor that works with girls who have eating disorders. Her name is Mrs. Smith. She is a young woman, very nice, and I think you would feel comfortable speaking with her. Mrs. Smith's office is located in her home, and there is a nice area where your little boy can play while you're counseling with her."

"How much would this cost? I don't have a lot of money, and without insurance I know this sort of thing can cost a pretty penny," I stated feeling this would all fall through because of the expense.

There had been other medical needs that I needed attended to at times since my divorce, but they went neglected due to having no money or insurance.

Reassuring my doubts she stated, "Like I said before, Courteney, don't worry about cost. Mrs. Smith will work with you on that issue. Let your thoughts focus more on getting better and taking control of your life."

Feeling a little relieved I answered, "Okay, I won't worry about the money issue."

"Before you leave today," she stated with a comforting smile and going on, "I want you to try and relax and feel that you have taken a big step. It's not easy admitting you have a problem. Most people spend their entire life denying their faults and wrong doings. It takes a strong person to take a good look at herself and admit she needs help. By speaking with you here today, I can tell you are a very strong person and have the desire and the will to get better. I know there is a lot of shame and embarrassment that goes with eating disorders, but in time you will learn not to be ashamed. You are a beautiful, young lady that has a lot to give in life. Now we just need to get you believing that," she said smiling.

"I want you to know that I am here for you as a nurse and a friend whenever you need one. I will help you with your nutrition and medical needs. Even if you don't have an appointment, stop in whenever you feel the need. Is that a deal?"

"Yes, it's a deal," I said returning her smile.

"Now, I know you probably have classes to attend today and a little boy to take care of. I won't keep you any longer," she stated handing me a business card. "This is Mrs. Smith's information. Give her a call, that is your next small goal we are setting for you," she said standing up. "Does that sound like a reasonable goal, and one that you are comfortable with?"

"Yes, I promise I will call her. There is a problem with the phone situation. I don't have a phone in my apartment. Is there anyway I could use your phone to call her?" I stated reluctantly.

"Not a problem, Courteney. On our way out you can use the phone."

"Thanks," I said standing up and following her out of the office.

Laying there in bed, I thought about the days events. The appointment with Nurse Nikki had given me some hope in my life. I knew it was going to take time to rid myself of this terrible illness, but the total strangers that were willing to help me were amazing.

"Lord, thank you for bringing Nurse Nikki into my life. I haven't met Mrs. Smith yet, but I'm hoping she is a lot like Nurse Nikki. Nurse Nikki is kind, easy to talk with, and most importantly, she doesn't think who I have become is stupid," I stated pausing to think about what I wanted to say.

"Lord, I start my first counseling session with Mrs. Smith in two days. Help me to have the courage I need to walk in there and speak openly and honestly with her. I know I have lied at length to my loved ones about my behaviors to cover up the shame and embarrassment I feel. I am sorry for not being truthful with them for so many years. Please forgive me, Lord. Maybe someday my parents will be able to forgive me for bringing shame to the family with this illness. I feel they are embarrassed by my illness, and I don't know how to make that better for them."

Rolling over onto my side, I wrapped my arm around my little boy. "Oh, and thank you, Lord, for this precious little boy you have blessed me with."

I started to think about Scott. I hadn't heard from him in so long. Tears started flowing and I quietly spoke, "Lord, please let Scott know that I am sorry for everything. Let him know that I love him."

Wiping away my tears, I gave my son a kiss and fell asleep feeling my faith in God was going to get me through the difficult times to come.

First Counseling Session

Sitting outside Mrs. Smith's house, I could feel chills overtaking my entire body. My body seemed to have this uncontrollable habit of trembling and feeling chilled whenever I became scared or uneasy with a situation.

Taking the keys out of the ignition, I sat there staring at Mrs. Smith's two-story, brick home. It reminded me of a house in Lawrence, Kansas, where Patrick and I went for dinner one evening.

Some of his college friends had invited him over to watch Monday night football and a pizza dinner. I wasn't much on watching football, but I figured hanging out with Patrick was better than sitting home by myself. It ended up being a great evening. Patrick and I ate dinner, but didn't spend much time watching football. We decided to go for a long walk.

It was a cool autumn evening, with a full moon to guide our way. We had one of our typical long talks about our future and dreams. He went on and on about becoming a doctor and wanting to help others. He was passionate about obtaining his goals, and I knew he would someday make a wonderful physician.

I still didn't know what my purpose in life was, and it worried me. Patrick sensed my worries and always tried to make me feel better. His words will forever stay with me.

"Courteney, just give it time. You'll figure out what you want to do with your life. You're an intelligent, strong young lady that can accomplish whatever you want. Sometimes it just takes people a little longer to figure out what they want out of life. I love you, Courteney, and will always be here for you," he said to me while giving me one of his warm and lingering hugs that I longed to feel.

Wiping away the tears that started to fall, I knew Patrick was here with me today while sitting outside of Mrs. Smith's two-story, brick home. "Patrick, I hope you are right about me being a strong person. I'm going to need every bit of courage I have to walk in this house. I'm so scared," I quietly whispered.

Lowering my head onto the steering wheel I silently prayed, "Lord, help me to have the courage to walk through those doors and start this journey. I am terrified of what lies ahead. I'm terrified Mrs. Smith will think my actions are stupid, or tell me there is no hope for me. Pausing for a moment to regain control of my shaking body, I continued, "Lord, only you know what lies ahead for me and where this journey will end. I trust that you will lead me on the right path."

Wiping away my tears, I lifted my head and glanced at the two-story, brick house. Sitting on the bird feeder in front of the house was a blue bird and a red bird. Smiling, I knew Patrick was truly with me in spirit.

Thinking back years ago, while on campus at Kansas University, I started to recall one beautiful spring day when Patrick and I were sitting around talking. Two birds, a red bird and a blue bird, were fighting over an earthworm. We found it humorous and even made a bet who would win the prize worm. We both won the bet, because the worm split into two pieces and both birds got their prize. The loser of the bet was to take the winner out for yogurt that evening. Since we were both winners, we decided it was only fair to go for yogurt Dutch style.

Sitting here watching these two birds at the feeder reminded me of Patrick and the love we shared. Smiling, I could feel myself calming down and knew that everything was going to be all right.

Looking into my rear view mirror, I could see Colby sleeping in his car seat. I hoped that he would be all right playing in a designated area, in a stranger's house for an hour. Mrs. Smith had reassured me that he would be okay. Her teenage daughter would keep an eye on him and help him if he needed anything.

Shaking his leg slightly I said, "Hey, sweetie, time to wake up."

Colby opened his sleepy eyes. Giving me one of his darling smiles he asked, "Are we there yet, Mom?"

"We are here. Are you ready to play with some toys?"

"Yes, I love playing with toys," he said excitedly unbuckling his own car seat and jumping out of the car.

"Slow down there, buddy," I said stepping out of the car and grabbing Colby's hand. "We need to watch for cars remember?"

Colby was getting ready to turn three years old and you'd think he had grown wheels on his feet. I needed a lot of energy to keep up with him.

Quickly glancing both ways he stated, "No cars, let's go."

While climbing the stairs to the front door, I stopped to observe the two birds at the feeder.

"Look, Colby. Look at the pretty blue and red birds. Aren't they pretty?" I said pointing at them.

"Yea, Mom, now let's go play with toys," he eagerly said while tugging at my arm.

At age three, he was definitely more interested in playing with toys than bird watching. I hoped someday he would learn to appreciate the beauty of God's creations.

"Hello, Courteney," stated a voice from the doorway. "You are Courteney Baker aren't you?"

"Yes," I said startled. "I was just admiring your birds at the feeder. I was showing them to my son, but I think he's more interested in playing," I said walking up to the doorway with Colby by my side.

Squatting down to be at eye level with Colby, she stated, "Glad to meet you, Colby. My name is Mrs. Smith. Would you like to play in the toy room with my daughter while I speak with your mother?"

Huddling closer to my leg, Colby started to revert back to his shy self.

"Yes, I like toys," he barely whispered.

"Great. Then follow me. I have the best building blocks in town. I have ones that are so big, I bet you've never seen anything like them, "stated Mrs. Smith with enthusiasm.

That definitely caught Colby's attention. Following her into the house he said, "You have really big, big blocks. I like to build."

Her teenage daughter was sitting on the floor watching television. You could definitely tell the two of them were related. If she hadn't introduced her as her daughter, they'd pass for twin sisters.

"Sandy, this is Colby. Colby, this is my daughter, Sandy. He's come to play for a little while. Would you like to show him our big blocks we have for building?" Mrs. Smith said to her daughter.

Smiling and coming over to greet Colby she said, "Hi, Colby. I've been waiting for you. I didn't have anyone to build with. Will you be my partner?"

Colby looked at me to see if it was okay. "You go ahead, Colby. I'll just be talking with Mrs. Smith," I said smiling and letting go of his hand.

Colby, hesitantly at first, walked with Sandy into the toy room. Once he saw all of the toys and blocks, he soon forgot about being in a strange house.

"Thank you, Mrs. Smith, for being so kind to my son."

"Not a problem. Sandy loves to play with the little ones; he'll be just fine with her. Why don't we go into my office and talk," she said leading me into a small cozy room.

Her office was a small room with a desk and two plush chairs. It was painted a soft yellow color and had a beautiful border trimming the top of the wall. The border reminded me of the dream home Scott and I always hoped to have one day together.

There were skyscraping snow capped mountains and a beautiful outdoor landscape with evergreen trees, a pond, and the most gorgeous little log cabin. The log cabin had smoke coming from its chimney and the sun was setting. The light of the sunset was pouring from the sky, painting the clouds and nearby mountains with a radiance that reminded me of how beautiful I thought heaven would be.

"I like the border," I said pointing to the wall.

"Thanks. It's one of my favorites too," replied Mrs. Smith.

"Why don't you make yourself comfortable, Courteney," Mrs. Smith said pointing to one of the chairs.

Sitting down in the chair, I started to feel unpleasantly cold and could sense my body starting to tremble slightly. I crossed my arms and started rubbing them to try and keep myself warm.

"Are you cold, Courteney? I could get you a blanket," Mrs. Smith stated sincerely.

"I think I'll be okay," I replied.

Mrs. Smith was a young woman, I'd say about mid-thirties, and very attractive. Her hair was a soft brown color, shoulder length, and curly. I've always liked curly hair, especially the spiral curl like hers. I had changed the style of my hair over the years to wearing it longer with the spiral curl. Our hair style was similar, but mine was about seven inches longer. She had a slender build and dressed fashionably. There was definitely a professional look about the way she dressed. Her tone of voice was very kind and patient. I was thankful for her kindheartedness she had shown so far.

Smiling at me she said, "Courteney, why don't you tell me about yourself."

I wanted to tell her I thought I was going to be sick, my stomach was doing flip flops, and I didn't want to go to the places her questions were going to take me.

Knowing I didn't have a choice if I wanted to get better, I took a deep breath and said, "My name is Courteney Baker, and I am twenty-three years old." Stopping for a minute to get control of myself I went on, "I am attending the education department at Missouri Western, and I am a single mom."

"You are divorced?" asked Mrs. Smith.

"Yes."

"How long have you been divorced?"

"For about a year and a half now."

"I have spoken with Nurse Nikki. She tells me that you are suffering from the eating disorder bulimia nervosa. Does your ex-husband know about this eating disorder?"

"Yes, he does."

"Even though you are divorced, is he supportive of you getting help?"

"I don't know. I haven't seen him since we've gotten a divorce. He is in the military and went to Germany about a year and a half ago. I haven't seen or spoken with him since. I have written to him, but I never get a response," I stated with tears starting to flow freely down my burning cheeks.

Handing me a tissue box she stated, "That must be difficult, especially with a little boy."

I just shook my head. I knew if I answered with words, I would start crying uncontrollably.

"Have you ever been to a counselor before, Courteney?"

Taking a deep breath to calm my nerves, I replied, "No, I haven't."

"Well, let me explain some things to you. Do you know what patient confidentiality is?"

"Yes, I think so," I said nodding my head.

"Great. Then you understand that anything you say to me stays between us. I will not use the information against you in anyway. The only way I would confide information to someone else is if you voiced any suicidal thoughts. Have you ever had suicidal thoughts?"

"I couldn't ever intentionally hurt myself, but there are times when I pray to God to just let me die from this illness. There are days when I just don't think I can go another day with the sadness and loneliness I feel inside."

"Do you have strong faith?" asked Mrs. Smith.

"Yes, I do. I didn't really understand how much I needed God in my life until I realized how sick I was and that this illness could take my life. When I realized that I had an eating disorder and became scared, God became more present in my life," I said wiping my eyes with the tissue.

"It is great to hear you have deep faith, Courteney. God will help you in your difficult journey. In fact, I think he has already helped you more than you know. Many people go through life denying they need help. You have taken on a huge responsibility by admitting to yourself you need help and coming here to speak with me today. You should feel very proud of yourself," she stated giving me a warm smile.

"Thank you," I replied trying to return her smile.

"I want you to understand that as your counselor, I will be asking you questions that will pry open doors that have been locked and secured for perhaps many years. We will be talking about your family, how you were raised, friendships, your relationship between your ex-husband and you, and many other aspects in your life that could be painful. When we talk, I want you to feel comfortable in opening up to me. I need you to be as honest as you can with how you feel about issues. You know, digging around in the past can be painful at times. But, it will help me understand more about you and how I can help you."

"I promise I'll try my best," I stated hoping I'd be able to keep that promise.

"I want you to do me a favor, Courteney. See the full-length mirror on the back of the door? I want you to walk over in front of it and tell me what you see. Be as honest as you can. Do you think you can do that?" she asked.

Her request threw me and I froze in sudden fear. I hated to look in the mirror. I didn't like what I saw.

"Do I have to stand in front of the mirror to answer the question? I purposely avoid mirrors. I can answer the question without standing in front of it," I stated feeling chills run through my body.

"Whatever you are comfortable with, Courteney," stated Mrs. Smith.

Taking a deep breath I started, "When I look at myself, I see someone who can't do anything right." Stopping for a minute to try and get control of my emotions, I continued on, "I see myself as having no control over my life. I have a tremendous fear of becoming fat, and I definitely don't deserve to be loved because of all my faults," I said starting to cry harder.

"I... I really try hard to be the person people want me to be, but somehow I always fail miserably."

"You say you have a fear of becoming fat. Do you feel you are fat now, Courteney?"

"No, I know I'm not big. When I was teenager, I felt a little overweight compared to other girls in my class, but I don't feel big now. I know I am a relatively small person. But I do fear becoming big."

"Why do you fear becoming big, Courteney?"

Jennifer Lynn

"I'm afraid if I become fat that I won't be loved like I would if I was petite. When I was a little girl I used to worry about getting big and my father not liking me anymore. His comments were never directed towards me, but when he would say things to my mother, I felt he wouldn't love me if I became big."

"What does he say to your mother?"

"He just makes comments to her while she's eating about how it will make her fat. He reminds her he doesn't like fat people."

"You said you try to please others, but you feel you fail miserably. Who is it you are trying to please all the time?"

"My parents, my ex-husband, everyone I love. It is important to me to please those that I love. I don't like to disappoint them."

"Let's start with your parents, Courteney. How do you feel you are failing or disappointing them?"

Pausing for a moment to think about the question I said, "Gosh, where do I start? There are many things about my life that don't seem quite good enough for my parents."

"Can you give me an example?" asked Mrs. Smith.

"Well, they didn't like the person I married. They'll tell you they like him, but Scott and I are two different people that come from two different worlds. My parents say he comes from an uneducated family that has different values and morals than our family. They tell me that I should marry someone that is well educated and comes from a better family."

"Scott is your ex-husband?" asked Mrs. Smith.

"Yes, Scott Linwood."

"Do you think your parents are correct? Do you think any less of Scott for not having a higher education or coming from a different type of family than your own?"

Tears started filling my eyes and I didn't know if I could answer that question. Staring at the floor, I finally managed to answer in a soft whisper, "It doesn't matter what I think anymore. I've lost Scott."

"It does matter what you think, Courteney. Your opinion is very important. Tell me what you feel from your heart, what you truly think of Scott. Not what your parents think," Mrs. Smith stated with a soft reassuring tone.

126

Grabbing another tissue and wiping my eyes, I finally found the courage to answer. "I don't think any less of Scott for not pursuing a higher education. He was a loving husband that cared very deeply for me at one time. We didn't have a lot of money, or a big fancy house, but it didn't bother me. Scott is a hard worker, and I thought we would make a good team. In the beginning of our marriage, the love and compassion we shared was amazing. As far as his family, well I don't see them much different than mine. They have great qualities and faults just like my family does. They were always pleasant to me and still are nice even though I am divorced from their son."

"What do your parents say about Scott since your divorce?"

"They reassure me how right they were about him. They told me when he left for overseas that he would just disappear, and Colby and I wouldn't see him again. They say he will be just like his father, because that is all he knows," I said softly crying.

"How does that make you feel?"

"It hurts."

"Do you tell your parents that it hurts you when they make comments like that?"

"No," I replied shaking my head.

"Why not?"

"My father will tell you he doesn't want to hear or talk about anything negative. When he is drinking, I hear that I am stupid for not seeing the true side of Scott. He'll tell me he's just like his father, and I'd have to be stupid not to see it. My mother usually tells me I am being disrespectful if I speak my mind. She tells me to move on with my life, to find somebody else that is educated."

"You keep mentioning Scott's father, and how they think Scott will be just like him. Tell me about Scott's father."

Pausing for a moment to think how to answer that question I replied, "Well, I don't have a close relationship with Scott's father. He's not disrespectful towards me or anything, just quiet. When Scott and I were dating in high school he always seemed unhappy in his marriage. Shortly after Scott and I were married, he left his wife for another woman. There was always talk that he had affairs, but I don't know how much truth there is to that. I never saw him with another woman. He was in the marines and served time in the Vietnam War. He definitely had a harsher tone of voice than I was ever used to growing up, and he was a strict disciplinarian."

"Courteney, I want to go back and talk about your parents. Do your parents know about your eating disorder?"

"Yes, they know about my eating disorder," I stated running my hands through my hair and letting out a big sigh.

"How do you think they feel about you having an eating disorder?"

"My dad told me my behavior was stupid; just to stop it."

"How does that make you feel when he says your behavior is stupid?"

"It's like a slap in the face, and the sting just never goes away. Bulimia has become so much a part of my life. It is a part of me just like my limbs are a part of my body. I want to let go and stop being bulimic, but I just don't know if I can. I'm afraid to let go, because I don't know who I am without this eating disorder. It's my escape when I get stressed or upset about something. Bulimia is the only way I know to get rid of the hurt and pain. If I try to explain this to him, he just says he doesn't want to hear it. He doesn't understand, but he should."

"Why should he understand?" asked Mrs. Smith.

"He drinks alcohol every night. He can't go for very long without his mixed drinks. He says he can stop whenever he wants, but he can't. He is lying to himself, just like I lied so many years to myself and others. He acts like he is doing nothing wrong, but yet my actions are stupid. I told him if he thought it was so easy, then to just stop drinking. My comment made him upset. He told me I was being disrespectful and to just get out of his house."

"Where do your parents live?"

"They live in Leavenworth, Kansas," I said reaching for another tissue.

"Do you see them often?" asked Mrs. Smith.

"Yes, they help with Colby. They are very active in his life. I appreciate everything they do with Colby. They take him on vacations that I can't afford as a single parent. My dad is great about taking him bike riding, hiking, swimming, bowling, you name it, he does it with Colby. There is a fun side to my father, but then when he gets drinking in the evenings it's another story."

"How is he different when he drinks?"

"Sometimes he says things that I feel aren't very nice. They are hurtful. Like I said earlier, he makes comments to my mother about her weight. She doesn't need to eat this or that because it'll make her fat. He is very vocal about not liking fat people," I said with anger in my voice.

"How does it make you feel when you hear him saying this to your mother?"

"Angry. I can remember him saying these words to her even when I was a little girl. I want to scream at him and tell him to be quiet," I stated with disgust.

"Do you tell your father how it makes you feel?"

"No, like I said before we're not allowed to. If there is any comment made against dad, we hear it from mom. We are being disrespectful. That is our father. He has done nothing but love us, put a roof over our heads, give us everything we want, and on and on."

"Are either of your parents overweight?" asked Mrs. Smith.

"No. My mother looks just like me. You can definitely tell I am her daughter. Sometimes people even have mistaken us as sisters. She is maybe ten pounds heavier than me, but definitely not big. My father has dark wavy hair, a mustache, and a small physique. We tease him sometimes by telling him he has bird legs."

"Do you have any brothers or sisters?"

"Yes, I have an older sister and a younger brother."

"Tell me about your relationship with them," stated Mrs. Smith.

"My brother, John, is autistic. I love him dearly, but we struggle with having a close relationship. He's not a person you can sit down with and talk with about life struggles, your dreams, and hopes for the future. He is a loving person, and would give the shirt off his back to a total stranger if he thought the person was in need. He loves to do for others, but it is just hard having a serious conversation with him."

"What about your sister?" asked Mrs. Smith.

"My sister, Kelli, is totally different than me in so many ways.

She is outspoken, wants to be in control, and will tell you how it is regardless if it hurts your feelings. When we were teenagers, we didn't get along very well. She was bossy and never wanted me to touch her belongings. Now, the relationship is better, but it still could use improvement. She is concerned about me and tells me she loves me a lot. She feels at a loss of what to do for me, but does want me to get better."

"You say you are totally different than your sister. How does that make you feel?" questioned Mrs. Smith.

"I guess I'm okay with being different than her. I would say the only thing that bothers me is not being able to stand up for myself when I know I should. Kelli doesn't let anyone push her around, and it seems pretty easy for her to stand up for herself. I'm always so afraid of hurting other people's feelings," I replied.

"Would you say your mother has a personality more like you or your sister?"

Smiling, I knew the answer to that question. "That's easy. My personality is like my mother's," I replied.

"Courteney, we are running out of time and I want to give you some valuable information before you leave today. The next time we meet, we will talk more about your relationships with family members, and work on issues. It is important for us to develop a plan to help you start getting better. Are you okay with this?" Mrs. Smith asked sincerely.

"Yes, that is fine."

"A person with an eating disorder has certain goals they need to accomplish to get better. You will be working on physical and psychological issues. The physical goals will include being able to eat a variety of healthy foods without bingeing and purging. Your desire to binge and purge will stay with you for a long time. When you feel the need to start the bingeing and purging cycle, we need to establish some healthier habits that can replace this behavior. What works for some people is to think of a safe place that your mind will allow you to go without feeling scared, anxious, stressed, or any of those negative feelings. It's a place that you can feel at peace. Everyone's safe place is different. Do you have any ideas where your safe place could be?" asked Mrs. Smith.

Staring at the floor, I tried to think where I felt safest. My mind started to envision the Trinity Episcopal Church in Atchison, Kansas. This is where Scott and I had been married.

Trinity is an attractive, Gothic style stone church that lies on the west bank of the Missouri River in the midst of the rolling bluffs. The nave is lit on either side by magnificent stained glass lancet windows that silhouette biblical symbols; enormous pipes climb the walls allowing beautiful organ music to pervade the church.

The high vaulted wooden ceiling, supported by black walnut trusses, has the symbolic appearance of an arc. The altar, which is enclosed by a brass rail, is beautifully carved white marble. The striking sculptured marble statue of Christ, which stands five feet tall in the center of the altar, never fails to capture my attention. Kneeling down before God with the Presence Candle burning fills me with a peace and security that I knew I would find only here in this church.

"I would have to say my safe place would be the Trinity Episcopal Church," I replied feeling confident with my answer.

"That's great, Courteney. This is one method you can use when you feel the desire to binge and purge. Try to relax and take your mind to your safe place. While you're at your safe place, think of all your strengths. Don't focus on your weaknesses. Stay at your safe place as long as time allows. I want you to try this and let me know how it works for you in a couple of days," she stated.

"I can do that," I replied. Hesitantly, I said, "I don't know... never mind."

"No, Courteney, go on. What do you want to say?"

"You said to focus on my strengths. I'm not sure what my strengths are," I stated feeling a little ridiculous.

"Your son would be a good one to think about. You seem very attentive to him, and he seems to love you very much. Think about the good times you have with him, and what a good mother you are being. You can also think about school, and all of the hard work you are putting forth to educate yourself. Don't forget about taking the necessary steps to help yourself. That takes a strong person, Courteney," replied Mrs. Smith.

"Okay, I'll try this method and let you know how it works," I stated understanding better what she wanted me to do.

"This strategy may work well one day, and not so good the next. Every new day, it will seem like new challenges surface. It can feel like you're on an emotional roller coaster at times. You can try other strategies to get through the urge to binge and purge. Find hobbies that will help you through those difficult times. What hobbies do you have?"

"I like to cook, sew, exercise, read, and listen to music," I replied.

"Cooking could be good or bad. As long as you are cooking healthy foods, that is okay. Cooking foods that you regularly binge and purge on is not such a good idea. Exercise is a good method, but you don't want to be excessive. You want to exercise in moderation for a healthy lifestyle. Music and sewing are two great hobbies that could be helpful. See if sidetracking yourself with hobbies will steer you away from your eating disorder. Do you like to write?"

"Yes, if it's something I have an interest in. I wouldn't like to write a paper on U.S. History, but there are topics that I do enjoy writing about," I replied.

"Have you ever heard of the word catharsis?" asked Mrs. Smith.

"No, I haven't," I replied feeling a little embarrassed.

"Catharsis is a technique that is used to relieve anxiety and tension. It is helpful in finding out what is really bothering you and understanding your feelings. The techniques used can vary from talking with a person, sharing with God, writing a letter or story, or keeping a diary. Do you do any of these already?"

"I share my feelings with God, but that is about it," I replied honestly.

"Talking to God is wonderful. What about writing? If you like to write, then I want you to start keeping a diary of your feelings. You can bring it with you to sessions and share it with me, or keep it private. The choice is yours. What matters is that you are getting your feelings down on paper and becoming more aware of your thoughts and feelings. Does that sound like something you would be comfortable with?"

"Yes, I think I could do that."

"You also said you liked to read. I want you to go to the campus library and check out books about bulimia nervosa. Educating yourself about the illness will help you in your recovery," stated Mrs. Smith.

Putting her pencil and paper down on her desk, she continued, "Your psychological goals for recovery will include trying to overcome the fear of becoming fat. Believing that you are a beautiful person whether you are big or small. What you are like on the inside is far more important than your appearance on the outside. You'll need to establish new coping skills, or you could say healthier habits, to help you through the tough times in life. Everyone goes through tough times; some just don't practice healthy habits to cope with those tough times. You need to replace your eating disorder with healthy habits. Does that make sense?" she asked sincerely.

"Yes, it makes sense."

"By what you have told me so far, it sounds like your mother and you have an emotional bond that hasn't been detached. You sound like a daughter that wants to feel close to her mother. It sounds like you've had different views on major issues concerning your life, and you are afraid of vocalizing that to your mother. When you have, it upsets her and then you back down fearing you will hurt her. Would you say there is some truth to that statement?" she asked looking at me for an answer.

Thinking about what she said for a moment, I stated, "Yes, I can say there is some truth to that. I am afraid to feel differently than her at times, because I know it will hurt her. I don't enjoy hurting her. I love her," I stated wiping away a falling tear.

"It sounds like you haven't ever formed your own being, Courteney. Who is Courteney? What do you want to do with your life? What beliefs and morals do you want to have and raise your children by? They don't have to be the same as your parents. They may not always agree with everything you do, and you need to learn to be ok with that. You can't please everybody all the time, including loved ones. These are issues we will work on together," she stated digging her calendar out of her desk.

"We have run out of time, and I am sure you are anxious to get home with your little boy," she said glancing at the wall clock.

"How often do you think we should meet?" I asked.

"Nurse Nikki told me you were bingeing two to four times a day, taking large amounts of laxatives, and then starving yourself for several days while exercising excessively. Is that correct?"

"Yes, that is correct," I replied.

"I think we should start with three times a week, until the bingeing and purging cycles slow down and it gets easier for you to work through them. When you feel like you are getting better we can reduce to two, and then one time a week. How does that sound?"

"That sounds fine," I said realizing all of a sudden that my insides had calmed down; I wasn't feeling ill anymore.

"Nurse Nikki informed me that you have appointments set up with her. She will be helping you understand the negative effects bulimia has on your body. She will also be giving you medical care to treat any physical effects you have acquired from the illness. She will counsel you on nutrition, and help design appropriate meals. It is equally important to keep your appointments with her as well as mine," she stated looking at me with sincerity.

"Yes, I have set up appointments with Nurse Nikki. I promise I will keep them," I replied.

"As far as pay, I quoted fifteen dollars a session to you on the phone. Is that going to be workable for you? I know money is tight."

"I'm fine with that amount," I said digging in my purse to pay her for this session.

"Do you want to do Monday, Wednesday, and Fridays the same time every day to start with?" asked Mrs. Smith.

"That's great," I said standing up to dismiss myself.

I started to walk out of her office, but suddenly felt I needed to tell her how much I appreciated everything she was doing for me. Turning around, I extended my arm and shook her hand saying, "Thank you, Mrs. Smith. Thank you for everything you are doing for me."

"You are very welcome, Courteney. Just remember to make

small goals for yourself. Those small goals will eventually allow you to reach your bigger goal. If you don't start small, you risk getting overwhelmed and falling back into the same vicious cycle," Mrs. Smith said standing up to walk me to the door.

That evening I decided to go for a walk with Colby and the neighbor's little dog. Colby wanted a puppy, but I just couldn't afford the extra expense. We had great neighbors that let us take their lively little puppy for walks whenever we wanted. They knew how much it meant to Colby.

"Colby, did you have a good time playing with Sandy?" I asked gently rubbing the top of his head.

"Yes, they have neat toys. Do I get to go back and play again?" he asked eagerly.

"Yes, we'll be going there quite a bit. I'm glad you like playing there," I stated feeling relieved that the experience would be enjoyable for him.

"Mom, where's my dad?" Colby asked.

Stopping to kneel down I said, "Remember I told you your daddy is in the military and is overseas right now." His question did not surprise me. He often asked me where his father was.

"Is he coming to see me soon?" he asked with a hopeful look on his face.

"I don't know, sweetheart. I truthfully don't know when he will be home again," I stated feeling the tears threatening to fall. Turning my face away from Colby so he wouldn't see me cry, I said, "Maybe we should take the puppy home now. It's getting late, and we need to get to bed."

"Okay, Mom. Will you tell me a story tonight about my dad?" he asked.

"Sure, sweetheart," I replied giving him a warm smile.

As we walked back to our apartment, I watched Colby happily playing with the neighbor's puppy. He didn't appear to be too upset with my answers about his father. I knew he missed his father, and I always kept a picture of him displayed in our apartment. I wanted Colby to know who his father was.

Sometimes when we went to bed, he would ask me to tell him a story about his father. I have found that his favorite story is the one about how his father flew all the way home from Korea on a big airplane just to see his baby boy being born.

It was hard answering Colby's questions about his father. Would Scott come home soon? When he did get back to the states, would he come to see us? I didn't know the answers to these questions, which made it even more difficult to answer Colby's questions.

I knew I needed to stop thinking about Scott. It would just get me upset and I'd wind up back in the kitchen starting the bingeing and purging cycle all over again. It was difficult not to think about him though, especially when Colby wanted to hear stories about him. I didn't blame him for wanting to talk about his father. It was only natural for him to be curious about his father since he never saw him.

We returned to the apartment and thanked our neighbors for the loan of their adorable Labrador puppy.

Colby was tucked into bed after a warm, soapy bath to wash off all of those puppy kisses that were smeared across his face. He must've been tired, because he fell asleep half way through the story I promised to tell him.

Giving him a kiss on the forehead I said, "Goodnight, sweetheart. I love you."

I settled myself on the front room sofa with a warm blanket. The fall evenings were getting cool, and I knew it would be only a matter of time before winter was here.

Reaching for the notebook and writing pen sitting on the coffee table, I started thinking about what I would write. Mrs. Smith had told me to keep a diary, a diary of my feelings. The day's events had taken a toll on my body. I was emotionally and physically drained. Deciding I was too tired to put a lot of thought into writing tonight, I decided I'd just write down my prayer. Those were my thoughts and feelings.

> Lord,
> Thank you for the little boy you have blessed me
> with. Give me the knowledge to know what to say to

him when he asks about his father. A little boy needs his father, and I just don't know what to do for him to fill that void in his life.

Thank you, Lord, for bringing Mrs. Smith, her daughter, and Nurse Nikki into my life. They truly are amazing people to go out of their way to help a total stranger in need. I hope their lives are blessed for the good deed they are doing.

Lord, I don't know where Scott is, or what he is doing, but could you watch over him. Keep him safe and out of harms way. I pray that he might write to us someday, or even better come to see us. Let him know that we miss him and think of him often. Help him to find it in his heart to forgive me for leaving him.

I'm going to need your help, Lord, in this journey I am undertaking. Sometimes I feel strong, but there are times when I am weak. I will think of you in those weak moments, knowing that you will give me the strength.

Amen.

Too tired to write anymore, I laid the pen and notebook back down on the coffee table. Pushing the button on my stereo, I could hear Kenny Rogers' voice filling the room. His voice definitely had a way of relaxing me, and I soon found sleep.

New Friendships

The winter's chill had arrived, bringing with it an ice and snow storm. I disliked the winter months. It made me nervous driving on ice and snow packed streets, causing me to confine myself to the apartment more. Even though I cringed at the sight of snowfall, Colby squealed with delight. It meant sleigh riding with Grandpa until his cheeks were rosy red, and afterwards enjoying Grandma's hot chocolate with tiny marshmallows to warm his insides.

"Is Grandpa here yet?" Colby asked eagerly running out of his bedroom. He was excited about going sledding with Grandpa. They thought it was perfect weather to go outside to play. I thought my warm apartment was the perfect place to hibernate.

"He'll be here soon. Be patient," I replied picking him up into my arms giving him a loving kiss and hug.

"Can I go outside and watch for Grandpa on the stairs?" he asked.

"It's too cold out there. Let's wait inside," I replied. Seeing the disappointment in his eyes, I stated, "Okay, just for a little bit. We'll have to put warm jackets on first."

While opening the hall closet to retrieve our winter jackets, I was never so happy to hear a knock at the front door. I dreaded the thought of having to wait outside in this freezing weather.

"Grandpa's here. Grandpa's here," Colby squealed with delight.

"Well, let him in. I'll get your overnight bag," I replied.

I could hear Colby opening the door, and starting to talk a mile a minute. He loved spending time with Grandpa. You would never know the child had a shy side to him the way he talked non-stop to family members.

"Hi, Dad," I said coming down the hallway.

"Hi, Courteney. How are you?" he asked holding Colby in his arms.

"I'm fine, Dad. Where are you going sleigh riding?"

"We'll probably go in Leavenworth down the hill from our house. What time do you want him home on Sunday?" he asked.

"Sometime between five to six o'clock would be good. Is that okay?"

"That'll be fine," he replied.

Handing him Colby's overnight bag I stated, "Hey, you need to give mom a hug and kiss good-bye before you leave."

Climbing down out of Grandpa's arms, Colby came over and gave me a quick hug and kiss. The kind that let's you know he has bigger and more important stuff to do than hugging and kissing.

"Slow down there, buddy," I said grabbing his hand. "You need your jacket on. Don't forget it is cold out there," I said teasingly. Slipping his little arms into his jacket, I pulled it snug around him and zipped it up.

"Keep your hood up. I don't want you getting an ear infection," I stated pulling the hood over his head.

Running back into Grandpa's arms, he stated with excitement, "Ready, Grandpa. Let's go."

"Thanks for having Colby for the weekend. You two have fun," I said walking them to the door.

"See you, Courteney," said Dad while walking out the front door with Colby in his arms.

I knew Colby would have a fun weekend. Dad was always the best at playing. He was like a little boy in a grown man's body.

Dad also had a tendency of buying Colby lots of toys while he was there. Colby never minded, but it bothered me some. I didn't want Colby thinking every time you walked into a store you got to buy something. Dad never told him no, and I feared he would get spoiled.

Shutting the door to keep the cold out, I headed down the hall-way to get cleaned up. Blake, my lab partner from Environmental

Biology class, was coming over tonight. We had to finish our lab assignment before Christmas break started next week.

Blake was a nice guy. He was also working on an Education degree with his certification for high school level. He played football for Missouri Western. Most people on campus knew him by his nickname, Red Beard. He had a stout build, soft red colored hair, and a short, red beard that complimented his looks. His goal was to be a high school teacher and to coach football. He had a passion for football, and I knew he'd make a great football coach someday.

I've been noticing that Blake has been going out of his way to do nice things for me lately. He's been walking me to classes and offering to carry my books. Living in the same apartment complex, he comes over often and takes Colby outside to play football. Sometimes he'll just stop by with a kid's movie and popcorn and hang out with us. I'm getting the feeling he would like to be more than just lab partners, but he hasn't verbalized his intentions in words.

Pulling a warm sweater over my head, I started to wonder if I would want to start a relationship with Blake. There were still so many problems in my life that I needed to work on. I was on this roller coaster journey trying to get my eating disorder under control. Since I had started counseling, I had good and bad weeks. It was a start. At least I was having some good weeks now. I was learning new strategies and behaviors to replace the bingeing and purging cycle.

I had found that having a private journal was helpful in understanding my feelings and what triggered the bulimia. I was sharing my thoughts with Mrs. Smith, but I wasn't sure if I wanted to share them with anyone else. Could I start a relationship with a man and give it my all? I had my doubts. Not only because of trying to rid myself of an eating disorder, but I still loved Scott.

Looking in the bathroom mirror to fix my hair; I decided it looked best with the sides pulled up in a barrette, and the back hanging down showing their spiral curl. Digging through my makeup bag, I touched up my lipstick with a soft rose color. Stepping back to check if my appearance was acceptable, I wondered why I was so worried about how I looked.

Did I want to start a relationship with Blake? I was lonely, and enjoyed his company. He was nice not only to me, but to Colby as well. Would he think I was crazy when he found out I had an eating disorder? Mrs. Smith had said that if I wanted to start another serious relationship with a gentleman that I needed to be honest with him. I needed to let them know I was battling bulimia. There were to be no more secrets and lying to cover up my illness. I guess I didn't need to worry about it unless the relationship changed.

Hearing the doorbell ring, I knew it was Blake. Taking one last glance in the mirror, I decided my appearance would have to be acceptable. I couldn't leave him standing out in the cold too long.

Heading down the hallway, I could feel butterflies fluttering around in my stomach. Usually, Colby was here when Blake came over. This would be the first time studying together alone.

Opening the door to let Blake in, I started to say, "Hi..." but stopped short.

"Hi there, Courteney," blurted out a drunken voice.

I recognized the guys face from campus and knew his name was Greg. He was well known on campus due to playing on the baseball team. The girls seemed to like him too, because of his good looks. He was tall, had dark tanned skin, and coal black hair. If you didn't know his personality, you'd take him as a very handsome guy. He lived in the same apartment complex and had thrown suggestive comments my direction many times. I ignored him, thinking he was pretty much a jerk. He didn't impress me with his good looks.

"Can't you say hello, Courteney?" he said with a harsh tone to his voice. Stepping inside my apartment without being invited he asked, "How come you never speak to me? You think you're too good for me or something?"

My entire body froze with fear. I would never have opened the door if I'd known it was him. I scolded myself for not looking through the little peephole to see who was outside the door first.

"You...you need to leave, Greg. You are not welcome here," I stated with a shaking voice.

"I'll stay if I want," he said grabbing my wrist and pulling me closer to him.

Tears started falling and my entire body started to shake uncontrollably. This couldn't be happening. I felt totally helpless. My body seemed to be immobile due to the fear that overtook me. His strength far exceeded mine, and I could feel a cold rush of panic rushing through my body.

"I think I will stay awhile. You and I will have a little party. What do you say?" he said reaching over to shut the door.

"No... No," I could barely choke out the words.

Just as he was shutting the door, I saw Blake's hand reach in to stop the door from going shut. He pushed it open saying, "Courteney, are you okay?"

I didn't have to say a word. Blake could see I was crying. He could feel the tension and fear that filled the room. He looked at Greg and saw him holding my wrist with a firm grip.

Putting his books down on the ground, he asked Greg, "What are you doing? I think you best let go of Courteney right now."

Knowing he was no match for Blake, Greg replied, "Just came by to say hello." Letting go of my wrist, he continued, "I didn't mean any harm."

"Talk to you later, Courteney," he stated with a tone that sent chills down my spine.

Blake watched Greg's every move as he stumbled down the stairs. When he was out of sight, Blake shut the door and locked it.

Turning around to face me he asked, "Are you okay, Courteney? Did he hurt you?"

With a trembling body I replied, "I'm okay. He didn't hurt me." Wiping away the tears with the back of my hand, I tried to get control of myself. Failing miserably, I started to cry even harder than before.

Blake walked over to me and put his arms around me. All the fear and anxiety that was trapped in my body came rolling out in tears. He let me cry until I couldn't cry anymore.

"I'm... I'm so sorry, Blake. If you hadn't shown up when you did, it scares me to think what could've happened," I said pulling myself out of his arms.

"It's okay, Courteney. Don't apologize for being scared and crying. He won't come here again. I'll catch up with him later when he is sober. I want to make sure he remembers my message when I have a talk with him," he said with a stern tone to his voice.

"I don't know if I'm in the mood to study now," I said still feeling shaky. What I really wanted was for Blake to leave so I could turn to my eating disorder for some comfort. I hadn't done anything all week, but the desire was growing stronger. I needed something to calm my nerves.

"We don't have to study right now, Courteney. We have all weekend to finish our project. You are trembling. Come sit down. I'll get you something to drink," Blake stated taking my hand and leading me over to the couch.

"I'll be fine, Blake. You don't have to stay."

Part of me wanted him to go, but the other part of me wanted him to stay so I couldn't do anything stupid.

"I'm not leaving you alone. Look how badly your hands are trembling," he said touching my left hand gently.

Our eyes met for a few seconds without a word being spoken. "Let me get you a blanket. You are trembling all over," Blake stated with concern.

"Thank you," I replied leaning back against the couch and closing my eyes. I needed to calm myself down.

I started to think about my safe place. A place where I could feel safe and no harm would come to me. The Trinity Episcopal Church was such a beautiful place. I thought about the statue of Jesus at the altar surrounded by the glow of flickering candles that represented the light of God. Kneeling down before the altar, I prayed, "Lord, please help me to calm myself down. The desire to turn to my eating disorder is strong. Help me fight the temptation."

Startled, I felt a blanket being laid over me. Opening my eyes, I saw Blake standing in front of me looking concerned.

"Are you all right?" he asked sitting down next to me.

Feeling a warm sensation flood my entire being, I replied, "I'm going to be fine. Thank you."

"I know you're not in the mood to study, but would you like to do something else together. We could watch a movie or go out to eat. My treat," he said with a smile while nudging me on the knee.

"Thanks for the offer, but I'm not in the mood to go out in this cold weather. I'd rather stay in where it is warm."

"Then we'll stay in and watch a movie," he said grabbing for the remote control.

"I'm not in the mood for television. I'd rather listen to music if you don't mind," I stated hoping he would be okay with the idea.

Placing the remote back down on the coffee table, Blake replied, "That would be great. We can listen to music and chat. We haven't ever had a chance to just talk and get to know one another. You know lab partners should know each other's life story," he said teasingly.

"I'll have to verify that information with the professor," I replied with a teasing smile.

Reaching over to turn on the stereo, I could hear Kenny Rogers' voice filling the room. "I hope you don't mind listening to Kenny Rogers. He's my favorite."

"That's fine," Blake replied.

The rest of the evening was wonderful. How I missed having someone my age to talk with. I enjoyed listening to Blake's humorous football stories that made me laugh until tears came. It was great experiencing tears of laughter rather than tears of sadness. It had been a long time since I had laughed that hard. I think he was purposely telling me humorous stories to help me forget what had happened earlier. It was working, and I appreciated his efforts.

"Enough of the humorous football stories," I stated holding my side. "My side is hurting from laughing so much. I don't think I can take much more," I said jokingly. "You haven't even told me where you are from," I stated.

"I'm from Columbia, Missouri. Have you ever been there?" he asked.

"Yes, I have. My father graduated from Missouri University. He has taken us there and told us stories of his college days. Why didn't you attend college there?" I asked curiously.

"I received a football scholarship at Missouri Western. When I finish college I plan on going back to the Columbia area. Hopefully, I'll find a high school teaching job and be able to coach football too," he stated.

"What about you? What are you going to do after you finish college?" he asked.

"I don't know. I don't have my life planned out like you do," I said teasingly.

"Seriously, tell me about yourself and what you think you will do," he said with a serious expression.

"Well, I'm afraid my stories aren't as humorous as yours. Truthfully, I haven't thought too much about my future and where I want to go after graduation." I paused for a moment to think about what I wanted to say.

"My life lately has been filled with a lot of pain and sorrow. I just try and make it from day to day hoping it will get better," I said looking away from him.

"I'm a good listener if you want to share," he said touching my hand gently.

Taking a deep breath and letting it out slowly, I finally got up the nerve to speak.

"If I tell you something about myself, you'll probably think I'm crazy," I said feeling the tears threatening to fall.

"I promise I won't think you're crazy," he stated sincerely.

I wanted to be honest with him. He was becoming a close friend. More than anything, I wanted to find a close friend. Someone I could trust and have long talks with like I used to with Patrick and Scott. There was so much shame and embarrassment that went with having an eating disorder. If I did tell him, I was taking a risk of losing a friendship that was becoming special.

With tears starting to fall, I finally told him. "I have an eating disorder. I am bulimic." Silence filled the room. I stared at the floor afraid to see his reaction.

Blake reached over and gave me a long hug. I tried to stop crying, but failed miserably.

Pulling back from me, he asked, "Courteney, are you getting help?"

Shaking my head, I stated, "Yes, I am. I am going to a counselor and getting nutrition counseling from the school nurse." Reaching for a tissue to wipe away the tears, I went on. "Nurse Nikki and Mrs. Smith have been great. They are doing so much for me. I'll have to admit it is a tough journey to travel. Some days are better than others. The bad days can get extremely difficult. There are times when I shake so badly trying to fight the desire to binge and purge. Sometimes I succeed in getting through those tough times, but there are times when I fail miserably."

Looking at him, I thought maybe I might have already said too much. He was sure to think I was crazy.

"I'm sorry. I shouldn't have told you all of this," I stated standing up to put some distance between us.

Grabbing my hand, he stated, "No, don't go away, Courteney, and don't be sorry. I'm glad you told me. Maybe I can be of some help. I don't know much about eating disorders, but I'd be glad to be here for you when you need someone to talk to. I definitely don't think you are crazy."

I glanced at our hands that were touching. I could feel my hands starting to sweat from being nervous by his gentle touch. I wondered if he noticed.

Sitting back down next to him, I said teasingly, "So you don't think I'm crazy. That's amazing, because there are times I wonder about myself."

"It sounds like you are taking the correct steps to get yourself better," said Blake.

"Thanks. I think I'm finally headed down the correct road of recovery. It is extremely difficult at times. Even though there are times when I want to give up, I don't. Colby is a big motivator. I want to be here for him. He means the world to me."

"I can see the love you have for your son. It's very special," stated Blake.

"Sometimes I feel like our love for one another is the only thing that keeps me going. I don't know what I'd do without my little boy. I am so blessed to have him."

"Not to change the subject, but were you married before?" asked Blake. Realizing that was a personal question, he went on. "I'm sorry. I shouldn't have asked such a personal question."

"That's okay," I answered. "I was married, but have been divorced for about one and a half to two years now."

"What is your ex's name?" asked Blake.

"His name is Scott Linwood. He is in the military and stationed overseas right now. Colby and I haven't heard from him for almost two years now," I answered.

"You haven't even received a letter from him?" he asked puzzled.

"No, not even a letter. If it wasn't for his parents, I wouldn't even know he is still alive," I stated sarcastically. Lately, I had grown disgusted with the fact that Scott didn't even make an effort to contact at least his son. He could hate me all he wanted, but it wasn't fair to punish our son for our failed marriage.

"That must be tough," he declared.

"The toughest part is watching Colby's curiosity about his father; knowing how to answer his questions about him."

"Colby seems like a happy little boy. You must be doing something right," Blake said squeezing my hand and giving me a warm smile.

"Thanks," I replied. "Well, you've found out that I'm divorced and battling an eating disorder. I have the makings for an interesting person. What do you think?" I asked jokingly.

"Actually, I think you are a very interesting person. You are obviously a strong person with a lot of determination. You have a lot you are trying to handle, and I think you are an amazing person. I guess I should mention that I think you are very beautiful too," he said with a soft tone.

I was surprised by his words, and turned away in embarrassment.

Sensing my reaction to his words, Blake stated, "I didn't mean to embarrass you. I have liked you for some time now. I just didn't know how to tell you, or know if you would be interested in me. Would you want to go out sometime, as a couple, not as lab partners?" Blake asked trying to throw some humor into the question.

Turning myself back towards Blake, I answered, "I would love to go out with you, Blake."

"Really?" he asked.

"Really," I answered with a smile.

Blake leaned over to give me a hug. "Don't forget that I am

here for you when you need someone to talk to about your eating disorder," he stated still giving me a long lingering hug.

"I won't forget," I stated giving him a soft kiss on the cheek. "Thank you for being such a good friend," I said pulling away from him.

"Are you in the mood for a movie yet?" Blake asked. "We could catch the late movie at the theatre if we hurry," he said glancing at his watch.

"That would be great," I replied.

Blake had succeeded in turning an evening that started off shaky into something wonderful.

A year had gone by since Blake and I started dating. I had learned a lot about eating disorders and shared this information with Blake. He was interested in my well being and tried hard to understand what I was going through. He told me many times that he didn't understand a lot of what I was feeling but respected my feelings. He never failed at being a good listener.

I still had a long way to go to be free of my illness, but slowly I was getting better. Prayer was still a daily ritual. In fact, I couldn't imagine going through a day without sharing my thoughts and feelings with the Lord.

Colby had just celebrated his fourth birthday. I had a birthday party for him with a few of his friends from school and family members. Blake came to his party too. Blake and Colby had developed a close relationship, but we always made sure that Colby understood that Blake was not his father. Blake was his buddy.

There were times when Blake would be walking across campus with us and people would stop and say, "I didn't know you had a son Blake." They didn't look alike, but the red hair always led people to believe he was Blake's son. We always corrected them.

Colby's curiosity about his father was growing stronger. I kept plenty of pictures of Scott around the apartment and told him stories about him. He loved the stories, but I could sense the hurt he felt from not being able to have a relationship with his father. It tore at my heart, but I was at a loss of what to do for him. It made it tough to fight my illness with this problem tearing at my heart.

I wasn't seeing Mrs. Smith as often as I did in the beginning. I went to talk with her about one to two times a month now. I had even attended a support group meeting several times that I thought was helpful. I found it interesting to meet other girls who were battling an eating disorder. Listening to their stories made me feel I wasn't alone in this tough journey. I was no different than a lot of other girls.

Mrs. Smith wanted me to talk to my parents about family counseling. She had informed me that the purpose of family counseling was to help the family and the sufferer to establish better relationships and change any unhealthy dynamics of the family. I knew my father wouldn't come to any counseling session. He always made it known he didn't want to hear anything negative, and he was sure to hear something at this session that he wouldn't be open to listening to. I knew mom would come, but I felt she would just be defensive. I had tried several times to explain to her about what I was learning about myself. She always disagreed with me. In her opinion, I was being disrespectful and blaming them for my illness.

I had developed friendships with others in the education department. Laurie, who was majoring in early childhood education, was one friend that I grew close to. Laurie was exceptionally striking in her looks. She was tall, slender, had long brown hair, and the most gorgeous smile. She was totally unaware of her beauty and, most importantly, had the kindest personality.

We discovered in our long talks that we had a lot in common. The love for talking was one of them, and we managed to have many long conversations.

I was drawn to her because of her deep faith in God. Our conversations consisted of how having faith in our daily lives was important. I had confessed to Laurie about my eating disorder, and she was yet another friend that filled my tough journey with positive comments and hope.

Picking up my personal diary, I started to think about what I wanted to write.

I wrote...

Christmas is just around the corner. I am actually looking forward to celebrating Christmas this year. The past few years have been hard not having Scott around for the holidays. I have come to the realization that Scott may not ever come back into our lives again. I am learning to accept that fact, and to move on with my life. I am thankful for all the new friendships I have acquired over the past few years. Blake and Laurie have especially become cherished friends that have brought a lot of hope into my life. I am thankful for their friendships.

I wish my parents would be more understanding of my feelings. They still make comments about Scott and how they knew he would just abandon us. It hurts to hear them say those words. I still have a hard time standing up to them. When I have tried to stand up for myself and how I feel, I am still told I am disrespectful. Am I being disrespectful? I'm still confused on what the answer to that question is.

My parents are wonderful with Colby and spend lots of time with him. I am grateful for all they do for him. I love them dearly. I just wish our relationship could be more positive. I feel like I walk on egg shells with them.

Blake has started casually talking about us getting married after we graduate from college. I care for Blake, and I do love him. I love him more as a friend though. It's not the romantic love that I felt for Scott. I don't give him an answer. He knows I still have feelings for Scott, and he says he understands. I don't want to hurt Blake. He has been such a good friend. This causes a lot of stress in my life. I just don't know what to do. I guess in time, I will discover the answer.

My eating disorder is getting better. I am so thankful. There are still times when I mess up and can't resist the temptation. Mrs. Smith tells me to keep making

those small goals even when I mess up. I remind myself
to be patient with myself. In time these small goals will
lead to my ultimate goal: being free of this illness.

The holiday season flew by quickly, and before you knew it we
were already well into the new year of 1993. Spring seemed to be
showing early signs of coming into our college town. I welcomed
its early arrival, hoping it would stick around for awhile.

"Mom, where are you going?" Colby asked curiously.

"I'm walking out to get the mail. Do you want to come?"

"Can I open the box with the key?" he asked.

"Sure, you can open the box with the key," I replied with a
smile.

Colby had this fascination with keys. He loved to lock and
unlock boxes, doors, or anything you could stick a key into.

You didn't have to walk far to get the mail. The mailboxes were
right across the parking lot. Grabbing Colby's hand to cross the
street, I reminded him to look both ways when crossing a road. He
always wanted to dart out across the street without looking.

"I know to look both ways, Mom," he stated with a big sigh.

"I was just reminding you."

"I'm big now. I can remember those things," he said standing
tall to show me how big he was.

"Yes, I suppose you are getting big now, Colby. You are growing
up too fast," I stated rubbing the top of his head.

Handing him the key to unlock the box, he stood on his tiptoes to reach the mailbox. He grabbed a handful of mail out of the
box and handed it to me. How I hoped there weren't a lot of bills.
Money was tight lately, and I always dreaded getting the mail. I
feared receiving bills I couldn't afford to pay.

Walking back to the apartment, I stated, "It's getting late. We
better get you ready for bedtime."

"But I'm not tired," he replied with a whiny voice.

"Sounds to me like you might be tired. Besides, I'm tired and
we have school tomorrow," I stated with a yawn.

After bath and a story, I tucked Colby into bed with a kiss and a hug.

"Goodnight, little one. I love you, "I said while giving him a motherly hug.

"I love you too, Mom, "he replied yawning.

Walking back into the front room, I saw the stack of mail still sitting there on the coffee table. I hadn't even looked at it yet. I knew I needed to sort through it before I retired to bed. Sitting down on the couch, I grabbed the stack and leaned over and turned on my stereo. Leaning back to get more comfortable, I started going through the mail.

About half way through the stack, I stopped and stared at a small, white envelope. I couldn't believe what I was holding. Tears started filling my eyes, and my hand that held the letter started to slightly shake. It was a letter addressed to Courteney, and the return address was from Germany. The letter was from Scott.

The Letter

I could feel my heart racing, and the tears were falling steadfast. I couldn't believe what I was holding in my trembling hands—a letter from Scott. For the longest time I stared at the white envelope, too afraid to open it and read the words that I waited so long to hear. Why had he decided to write after three years of not hearing a word from him? I wanted to rip it open and take in every word, but there was a part of me that was scared of what he had to say. Maybe he was writing to let me know he had gotten remarried.

Grabbing a tissue to dry my eyes, I knew I had to get control of my emotions. Taking a deep breath, I started to slide my finger under the seal and rip it open. The letter didn't feel thick. Scott wasn't much on writing, and I figured he probably wrote everything he had to say on one page. There was one sheet of military green paper folded in thirds in the envelope. Slowly, I pulled it out and unfolded it.

Scott wrote:

> Dear Courteney,
>
> I hope that Colby and you are doing well. I know it has been a long time since you have heard from me. You are probably pretty upset with me by now. I won't try to make excuses for myself. My actions were the only way I knew how to deal with the hurt and pain I have felt since I left for overseas.
>
> I have thought about the two of you everyday and prayed that you were getting the help you needed with

your eating disorder. I have no doubts that you and your parents have taken good care of Colby.

I am writing to ask you and Colby to move to El Paso, Texas with me when I get back to the states. I will be stationed at Ft. Bliss. I love Colby very much and want to get to know my son. I'm not sure how you feel about me, but I still do have feelings for you. I would like to see if our relationship could be saved.

We wouldn't be leaving for Ft. Bliss, Texas until mid-May. If you are still in school you should be able to finish the semester before we would leave. This will also give us some time together to get to know each other again.

I fly into the Kansas City International Airport on March 26, 1993 at 3:10 p.m. I would love to have the both of you there when I arrive at the airport. If you choose not to be at the airport when I arrive, I would understand. I don't know if you have committed your-self to someone else. It is your choice.

Love, Scott Linwood

I couldn't believe what I had just read. I read it a couple more times to make sure I didn't misunderstand anything written. Scott was coming home, and he wanted us to move to Texas with him. I was excited about this news. Getting up from the couch, I didn't feel tired anymore. In fact, I was having doubts if I would be able to sleep until his plane arrived into Kansas City.

The feeling of excitement disappeared quickly when I started to think about how others in my life would respond to this news. How would this effect Blake? Blake had become a close friend, and I didn't want to hurt him. He had been a tremendous help through some of my rough days while struggling with my illness. We had formed a close bond over the past year. I did love him, but as a friend.

My parents were another couple of people that I would dread telling the news about Scott's letter. I already knew what their response would be. They would be angry if I moved away to Texas with Scott. I'd probably get the response of how stupid my actions would be. How I would be only thinking of myself, not my son.

I grew more frustrated as I thought about what my parents' response would probably be to Scott's letter. Starting to cry out of frustration, I lay down on my bed and wept until I heard Colby stirring around.

It was morning, and I hadn't slept a wink. My face was swollen from crying, and my desire to turn to my illness was strong. What was I going to do? I couldn't call Blake and ask for his help. I wasn't ready to tell him about Scott's letter yet. My choice was not wise nor did I think about the consequences that went with my actions. For the next two weeks I fell back into the same old cycle of bingeing, purging, and fasting.

I avoided the mirror once again, not liking what I saw in its reflection. I felt miserable, depressed, sick to my stomach, and once again not in control of my life. I was failing my son and most importantly myself. I tried to turn to some of the strategies that Mrs. Smith had taught me in our sessions, but I was failing miserably at everything I tried.

Blake had called and stopped by the apartment many times, but I always had an excuse for him. I was managing to attend most of my classes on campus, but came home directly from school. I was even avoiding my girlfriend, Laurie. It was only ten days before Scott came home, and I needed to get control of myself and decide where my future would be. Is my future with or without Scott?

I finally decided I needed Mrs. Smith's help and gave her a call. We set an appointment up for that afternoon. I told her it was an emergency and needed to talk with her right away. I planned on reading Scott's letter to her and discussing the impact it had on my eating disorder. For the longest time I was doing so much better. Now I felt totally out of control and didn't know how to get back on track.

I was more than anxious to get to Mrs. Smith's house and talk with her. I knew she would be understanding, and would listen to what I had to say without being judgmental. I scolded myself for not thinking of calling her earlier.

Sitting down across from Mrs. Smith, I started digging Scott's letter out of my purse.

"Are you okay, Courteney? You don't look like you feel too well," Mrs. Smith asked with concern in her voice.

"I'll be honest with you. I haven't done well with my eating disorder for the past two weeks. I have been very sick from bingeing and purging," I stated feeling ashamed of my actions.

"Tell me what is going on, Courteney. What has happened that has thrown you back on the wrong track?" Mrs. Smith asked.

Holding Scott's letter in my hand, I said, "This letter. I need to read it to you."

I took out Scott's letter and read it aloud to Mrs. Smith. After I finished I asked, "What do you think? What should I do?"

Smiling, Mrs. Smith answered, "Courteney, I cannot tell you what to do. It is your life, and you need to decide that for yourself. But, I will help you through your feelings about this letter and what Scott wants of you."

Feeling a bit disappointed, I replied, "But, I don't know what the right answer is. I will hurt a lot of people if I do what I want to do."

"This is what we have been working on all along, Courteney. You need to decide for yourself what you want out of life. What do you want, Courteney? What is best for you and your son? Those are questions that you will need to answer for yourself. Who are you afraid of hurting?" Mrs. Smith asked.

"I know my parents will be the most upset," I replied.

"Have you mentioned it to them yet?"

"No, I haven't."

"First, let's talk about what you want. What are your thoughts? What do you want?" Mrs. Smith asked sincerely.

"I still love Scott. More than anything I want to be with him. Maybe my mother is correct about us being too different for one another. Maybe it just won't work and I am being stupid in my thinking," I replied with tears starting to fill my eyes.

Handing me the tissue box she replied, "Remember when I told you about my husband and I. I used our relationship as an example. We are totally different people, and we have a strong marriage.

A marriage can work if you have honesty, trust, and teamwork. Do you remember when we talked about that?"

"Yes, I remember. I doubt myself at times though," I replied drying my eyes with a tissue.

"In time, you will get stronger and stop doubting the way you feel. It just takes time and patience. Listen to what your heart is telling you and trust your instincts," Mrs. Smith said.

Staring at the floor, I thought about what Mrs. Smith had said. If I follow my heart, I was sure to hurt a lot of people.

"You want to share your thoughts?" asked Mrs. Smith.

"I was just thinking that my heart tells me that I love Scott. I still to this day can not imagine my life without him. I think Colby needs his father. I think all three of us need one another," I stated with tears rolling down my burning cheeks.

"Then let that be your decision," Mrs. Smith stated with such ease.

"But there is still the issue of my parents," I stated feeling my stomach being tied in painful knots. The thought of having to tell them was more than I could handle.

"If your parents are upset by the news, then you will have to just let them be upset, Courteney. Just reassure them that you love them, but this is your life and you need to do what you feel is right. In time, they will come around because they love you," Mrs. Smith stated with such confidence. I hoped she was correct. I hated to disappoint my parents, and wanted their love and acceptance more than anything.

"You wouldn't by chance want to come with me when I tell them would you?" I asked teasingly.

Smiling, she replied, "You're on your own, Courteney. You have to learn to stand up for what you want in life. You need to make your own decisions. Remember, your parents may not always agree with your decisions and you need to learn to be okay with that. Some of the decisions in your life will turn out good, and some will not turn out so good."

"What if my decision to get back with Scott turns out to be a bad decision? I don't want to do the wrong thing," I stated with a worried tone to my voice.

"Courteney, that is how people learn and grow in life. Everyone has to make choices. Some decisions we make turn out good, and some turn out bad. Both teach you lessons and help you grow as a person. Do you understand that?"

"Yes, I do."

"Are you still praying and asking God for guidance?" Mrs. Smith asked.

"Yes, all the time. The Lord probably thinks I talk way entirely too much," I stated teasingly.

"The Lord would rather hear your voice often than not at all. Just keep on praying," she stated with a smile.

"You stated earlier that you have turned to your eating disorder the last couple of weeks. Why do you think you have done that?" Mrs. Smith asked.

"I guess because I am a nervous wreck about telling my parents about Scott's letter and what I want to do," I stated. Stopping for a minute to collect my thoughts, I continued on, "I've tried thinking about my safe place, listening to music, and writing my thoughts down in my private journal. Nothing seems to be helping like it used to. Why?" I asked confused.

"This is a big decision that causes a lot of stress and anxiety for you, Courteney. It will take time, patience, and determination to work through the difficult times without ever turning to your eating disorder again. You will have weak moments. Don't get discouraged or beat yourself up over it. Tell yourself you can do it, and have patience with yourself. You can do this, Courteney," she stated reaching over to touch my arm. It was a simple touch that gave me a feeling of reassurance.

Feeling the tears threatening to fall again, I replied, "You're right. I can do this. I'm sorry if I have disappointed you with my actions."

"You haven't disappointed me at all, Courteney. Remember in the beginning I told you this journey would feel like a roller coaster. You will have ups and downs. Get back on track, and don't beat yourself up over your fall. I know you can do this," she stated with sincerity.

"Thank you for everything. Especially all of your kind words, and believing in me. I just thought of something. If I move to Texas, I won't be coming to see you anymore," I said sadly.

"Yes, I had thought about that. I still think you need to counsel with someone about your eating disorder. You have come a long way, but you still have a long ways to travel on this journey. You will need help. Promise me that you will find a counselor and perhaps some support groups if you do decide to move away," Mrs. Smith stated.

"I promise I will find someone to counsel with," I replied.

"Remember when you find another counselor, they may have different strategies than we have talked about. Always remember that if you don't connect with a counselor, there are always others. Find someone you are comfortable with and feel free to tell your feelings to. Be open to new ideas," Mrs. Smith stated.

"I will keep that in mind," I replied.

The thought of not being able to talk with Mrs. Smith again if I moved away saddened me. She and Nurse Nikki had been a blessing, like angels sent from the Lord to help me through this difficult time in life. How could I ever repay them for what they were doing for me?

Trying to choke back the tears I stated, "Mrs. Smith, I hope you understand how much I appreciate everything you have done for me. Even though I hate this illness and it has brought so much pain, I am thankful for everything you have done."

"I know you are, Courteney. We are running out of time, and I want to leave you with these words. You may not understand fully what I am saying now, but in time you will." Pausing for a moment to collect her thoughts, she continued, "In time you will learn not to hate your illness. Not to feel the shame and embarrassment you feel with it now. In time you will see that you have been given a special gift. You have determination, compassion, and strong faith. Keep praying and listening to what the Lord has planned for you. Follow what your heart tells you," she stated with confidence.

Standing up to leave, I replied, "Thank you. I will think about what you said."

Lying in bed that evening, I started to think about Mrs. Smith's words. I wasn't so sure about learning to not hate this illness. She says I will learn to not feel ashamed and embarrassed. I had my doubts. She was probably just being nice. She hasn't ever had an eating disorder that I knew of and just didn't understand the feelings that go along with it.

I definitely didn't understand how she thought my illness was a special gift. In no way did I think it was special. It brought so much shame and embarrassment to the family. I wanted to be rid of this so called "gift" and erase that part of my life permanently.

I did understand and agreed with her about having determination and strong faith. Being strong willed and having determination was working to my advantage in my journey of ridding myself of this eating disorder. I was undeniably determined to beat this illness.

Feeling exhausted by the days events, I knew I needed to take the time to pray about my decision and what the consequences could bring.

"Lord, thank you for all the blessings you have given me. Especially my adorable little red head that brings so much joy to my life. I've been feeling a lot of anxiety lately. Scott has written to me and wants us to move to Texas with him. I love Scott, Lord, and can't imagine my life without him. I have decided to go with him, but I know my parents will be upset. Well, probably more than upset. They will be down right angry with me. Please help them understand and to forgive me for hurting them. Help me to have the courage to tell them and to stand up for what I feel is right. I know that Scott and I will have a lot of difficult issues to work through. Help us to get past the hurt and to forgive our wrong doings. Help me to get control of my eating disorder. I don't want it to have control over me. I hate having this illness, Lord, and I want to be free of it. Mrs. Smith says in time I will understand I have been given a special gift. I don't understand. How can my eating disorder be a gift?"

Drifting off to sleep, I felt at peace with my decision.

It was only a few days before Scott arrived at the airport, and I still hadn't told my parents about Scott's letter. I had talked with Blake, and he surprisingly understood. We both agreed that our relationship would have to change, but we would always cherish the friendship we shared. I knew Blake would always have a special place in my heart. The kindness he offered to my son and I and having a shoulder to cry on through such a difficult period of time in my life will never be forgotten.

Colby had no idea his father was returning home. I had decided to wait until he arrived, just incase something happened and plans changed. I didn't want to tell him he would be seeing his father and then disappoint him. Colby knew what his father looked like by the pictures I had up in the apartment. I didn't know if Scott still looked the same as he did three years ago or not. I was getting a little nervous if even I would recognize him after such a long separation.

My dad was going to take Colby out for another one of their adventurous days of hiking and biking. I thought I would take this opportunity to talk with my mother about what was getting ready to happen. I knew I wouldn't be able to talk to dad about it. It was mom I would have to tell, and then she would inform father of my decision.

Driving over to their house to drop Colby off, I kept going over in my head the best way to tell mom about Scott's letter. Every plan I came up with seemed inappropriate or just an all around bad idea. I thought about taking her out to lunch and telling her, but I didn't want to cause a scene in a restaurant. The thought occurred that we could spend the day shopping, maybe get her in a good mood, and then talk with her. I was always in the mood for a great day of shopping but doubted I would have much fun. I wouldn't be able to enjoy myself knowing what was coming at the end of our day.

I finally decided that as soon as Colby and dad left the house, I would just get it over with. I was going to sit her down and read Scott's letter. It was a given she was going to be mad and have her opinion. She was entitled to that, but she was going to have to accept my decision. At least I hoped and prayed she would forgive me someday for not feeling the same way she did.

Pulling into the driveway, I saw dad sitting on the back porch waiting for our arrival. He immediately stood up and came over to greet his grandson.

Opening the car door, he asked, "Hi there, Colby. How are you today? Are you ready to go bike riding?"

"Hi, Grandpa," Colby squealed with delight. "I'm ready to go ride bikes."

Picking Colby up into his arms, he stated, "Well, let's get going then. We better go say hi to Grandma first though. She'll be upset if you don't come in and say hi to her."

"Okay, but let's hurry. I want to ride my bike."

Dad started walking off with my son in his arms without even a single word spoken to me. I grabbed my purse and followed the two of them into the house.

"Hi, Dad," I said closing the door behind me.

"Oh hello, Courteney. We're just going to find Grandma real quick and then we're heading out. Do you mind if Colby spends the night tonight?"

"No, that is fine. Just have him home tomorrow by six o'clock in the evening. Is that okay?" I asked.

"Sure, that's fine. Now let's go find Grandma," Dad said to Colby as they started roaming through the house yelling for her.

My stomach was doing flip flops, and I knew it was only going to get worse when I actually sat mother down to talk with her. I decided a little fresh spring air would do me good.

I took off walking around the block. Taking deep breaths and letting them out slowly always seemed to help calm my nerves. About half way around the block I saw two birds that caught my attention. It was a red bird and blue bird. These two birds always triggered thoughts of Patrick and gave me a feeling that he was with me. Smiling, I knew I was not alone.

Sitting down on the cool, damp grass, I watched the two birds fluttering around in the trees. "Patrick, I am nervous about telling my mother about Scott's letter. She will not agree with my decision to reconcile with him. How I wish you were here so I could have a shoulder to cry on when this experience is over with. I have a feeling I'm going to need a friendly shoulder. Oh, and by the way. I miss you and love you lots," I said with a single tear trickling down my cheek.

Wiping away the tear, I knew I needed to get back to the house. I figured the two bikers were already gone for the day. I didn't know if mom had other plans, but I sure didn't want her taking off anywhere before I had a chance to speak with her.

Walking back into the house, I heard mom yell, "Courteney, is that you?"

"Yes, it's me," I hollered back.

"I'll be right down. I'm just finishing up doing my hair."

"That's fine," I replied. I started to dig through my purse to retrieve Scott's letter.

Walking down the stairs, mom asked, "What do you have planned for the day, Courteney?"

"Not a whole lot. I'll probably work on homework and perhaps do some cleaning at the apartment."

"Is your illness getting better, Courteney? Are you still going to counseling?" she asked.

"Yes, I still go to counseling. I'm learning a lot about my illness, and I am making progress," I replied.

"Do you want to go shopping together today?" Mom asked.

"Maybe later. I need to talk to you about something first," I stated feeling like my stomach was being twisted into knots.

"This sounds serious," she said giving me one of her worried looks.

"It is a serious conversation, but don't worry. I'm not dying or anything," I said jokingly trying to relieve some of the tension that was building.

"Does this conversation have anything to do with your eating disorder?" Mom asked.

"No, it doesn't. It has to do with Scott," I replied hesitantly.

Scott's name grabbed her attention. "What about Scott?"

"I heard from Scott," I replied with barely a whisper.

"You talked with him on the phone?" Mom asked with a bit of sarcasm in her voice.

"No, I received a letter from him."

"It's a little too late for a letter, don't you think?" Mom asked.

"Mom, I want to read the letter to you. Do you want to hear what he has to say?" I asked.

"I guess. If you want to share it with me, go ahead," she replied.

"Before I read it to you, I want to ask you to not say a word until I read the entire letter. Okay?"

"This must be a letter I'm not going to like hearing. Okay, I promise."

I started to read the letter to her. My hands were shaking so badly, I had to lean against the kitchen counter to steady them. I wondered if my mother noticed how nervous I was.

When I came to the part about moving to Texas she broke her promise.

"I can't believe the nerve of him. Move to Texas! Does he really think you are that stupid?" she asked.

"Mom, you promised not to say a word until I finished the entire letter," I stated.

Shaking her head disgustedly, she replied, "Okay. Finish the letter."

I read the rest of the letter to her and then folded it carefully back up. I was scared to look her straight in the eye. Her expression on her face was one I didn't care to see.

"Well, Scott sure has a lot of nerve writing you after three years and expecting you to pick up and move to Texas with him. Once again, he's only thinking of himself. If he cared about the two of you, he would've been writing and coming to see you when he could," she stated with anger in her voice.

Tears started forming in my eyes. I knew I wasn't going to get through this without crying. I still couldn't look directly at her, fearing the argument that was going to arise from my decision.

Sensing my uneasiness, she asked, "Courteney, what are you going to tell him? You surely aren't going to go to the airport to meet him are you?"

Tears were flowing freely, and I wanted to run to the bathroom and be sick. I couldn't control my shaking body.

"Courteney, answer me. You aren't going to the airport are you?"

"Yes, Mom, I am going to the airport to meet Scott," I replied with barely a whisper. Turning away from her, I didn't think I was going to get through this conversation without being sick.

"Don't turn away from me, young lady. After everything your father and I have done for you, and now you betray us like this. You are the most disrespectful, spoiled brat I have ever known," she said screaming. Coming around in front of me she continued on, "You're planning on moving to Texas with him aren't you?"

I was too afraid to answer, and was crying so hard that words would've been impossible.

"Answer me, Courteney. Are you planning on moving to Texas with Scott?" she screamed with such anger that her body was shaking.

I covered my wet, hot face with my hands. I knew this wasn't going to be easy, but it was ending up far worse than I ever imagined. I tried to think about what Mrs. Smith had told me. I needed to stand up for what I felt was right. My parents didn't have to agree with me, and I needed to learn to be okay with that.

Taking a deep breath, I finally replied, "Yes, Mom. I am planning on moving to Texas with Scott."

"Courteney, I can't believe what I am hearing. I thought you had matured over the last few years and gotten smarter about life. You still are making such stupid decisions. What about your son? Are you even thinking about him? He doesn't even know his father. This is not in the best interest for your son. You are only thinking of yourself," she stated angrily turning away from me.

Sobbing through my words, I replied, "Mom, I am thinking about my son. He needs his father. I want to give that to Colby. I want him to know his father and get to spend time with him."

"It won't last, Courteney. If he even does show up, it'll be for a short period of time. He'll get tired of you two hanging around then be off again. He's just like his father, Courteney. Don't you see that?" she asked.

"No, Mom. I don't see that in Scott. That's not why we divorced in the first place. I left him remember. Scott didn't take off on me. Scott was heartbroken when I left him. A lot of our problems were due to my lying to cover up my illness. There were other issues too, but I hold just as much fault in our failed marriage as Scott does."

Throwing her hands up in the air, she stated, "This is crazy, Courteney. Scott disappears for three years without a word. We go out of our way to help you with your son, our grandson, and now you want to take him away from us. That is the thanks we get. We'd been better off not doing anything for you. Maybe you would treat us nicer."

"I am not trying to hurt you, Mother. I need to do this for Colby and me. I believe Colby needs his father. I also love Scott and still to this day cannot picture my life without him. I have made a lot of mistakes in the past, and I am giving it my all to try and correct those mistakes. My eating disorder is one of the biggest mistakes I have made. It took over my life, but I am trying to take control of my life now. If I don't try to work things out with Scott, I will always wonder if it could've worked. Please try to understand," I said trying to calm my tone down. I didn't want this to be a screaming match.

Turning to face me, mom said with a firm tone, "Understand this, Courteney. If you go to Texas with Scott, I am through with you. I don't care what happens to you. The only person I will worry or care anything about is our grandson. I am through with you. Do you understand me?"

She just stood there staring at me waiting for an answer. Starting to tremble, I finally answered, "Yes, Mother, I understand."

She stormed out of the room madder than a hornet. I didn't figure she would be speaking to me for a while. I could feel the anger building inside me and knew I needed to get out of the house. I grabbed my purse and car keys and headed out the door. I had no idea where to go, but I knew I couldn't stay there.

I drove around for several hours not knowing where to go and crying non stop. The more I thought about her words, the angrier I became. What was I going to do? I stopped by a couple of friends houses in North Kansas City, but nobody was home. I needed someone to talk to. The desire to turn to my eating disorder was strong. I was feeling out of control, and didn't know what to do to gain that control back.

Sitting in the parking lot of my friends' apartment, I finally decided I couldn't handle it anymore. I'd cried until there were no more tears. My face was swollen, I had a headache, felt sick to my stomach, and my body was shaking uncontrollably. I decided to drive around and find a grocery store. I could get everything I needed there to relieve the anxiety I was feeling.

Luckily, I didn't have to drive far. About a block away was a large grocery store where no one would recognize me. I didn't care if they thought I was strange buying huge amounts of junk food and a box of laxatives. At my hometown, I would always go to several grocery stores so no one suspected what I was doing.

It didn't take long in the store to grab the items I needed. When I returned to my car, I sat everything in the front passenger seat. I had already decided that I would drive home, and binge the entire way there. Starting the car, I grabbed a bag of donuts and ripped it open.

Before I could take that first bite that was sure to lead to disaster, I heard a familiar song fill the car. It was the song, "I'm Sorry," by John Denver. I had recently seen John Denver in concert in Branson, Missouri at the Grand Palace. This was one of my favorite songs of his. I remember crying and thinking of Scott while John Denver sang this beautiful song.

Leaning my head back against the headrest, I closed my eyes and took in every word of the song. His voice had a way of calming me down and gave me a feeling of peace. Tears were streaming down my face.

Why am I doing this? I don't want to. Scott will be home in a couple of days, and I want to feel good. I didn't want to be sick from a binge and purge episode. I knew I needed help.

"Lord, please help me. I don't know what to do. Where do I turn for help? I want to get better, but this is so difficult. I feel like I'm coming out of my own skin. I need you now more than ever before. Please help me get through this," I said crying softly.

Glancing at all the food and laxatives on the car seat, I just shook my head in shame. "I can't do this," I stated, talking to myself.

I started thinking of the Trinity Episcopal Church in Atchison, Kansas. This was my safe place that I let my mind escape to when I needed help. Maybe I could drive there and someone would be at the church that I could talk with. It was worth a try. At this point I was feeling desperate and would try just about anything.

All the way to Atchison, I listened to music and tried to keep my mind off of the items sitting in the seat next to me. I didn't trust myself. I needed to get the items out of the car. When I approached the bridge that crossed the Missouri River, I thought about where I could dispose of the junk food and laxatives. When we were teenagers, we use to go down to the river and hang out by the caves. I decided it was the perfect spot to dump these unwanted items that would lead to another episode. The fish in the river would surely enjoy eating all of the food. I would dump the laxatives in a trash barrel at the gas station.

I stopped at the gas station just before crossing over the Missouri River into Atchison. After dumping the laxatives into the barrel, I headed over the bridge down to the river by the caves. Grabbing the grocery bag full of food, I walked over to the bank of the river. The river was high from all the spring rain we were having. I didn't hesitate when dumping the laxatives, but for some strange reason dumping the food items took a little longer.

As I was standing alongside the Missouri River, watching the whirlpools, .I realized this was the first time I had ever stopped myself from bingeing and purging after purchasing the supplies I needed. Usually, I carried through with the act if I had bought the food and laxatives. There was no doubt in my mind what I needed to do.

Opening the bag, I grabbed a handful of food and started throwing it as far out into the river as I could. The tears started falling, and by the third handful I was screaming as loud as I could with each handful thrown. All of the anger that was buried deep inside me was coming out. I hoped that no one was around to observe my actions. They surely would think I was crazy.

Putting the trash in the trunk of my car, I headed to the church. It wasn't far from where I was. When I pulled into the church parking lot, I didn't see any vehicles. Walking up to the church door, I pulled on the handle to see if it was locked. Unfortunately, it was. There was no one here, but I wanted to stay. There was no one around, and I didn't figure anyone would bother me here.

Walking into the church garden, I laid down on the cool, green grass. The garden was beautiful with its flowers in bloom and the charming statue of St. Francis. The center of the garden had a Celtic cross with burial sites surrounding it. The sun was starting to set, and the suns rays were turning the horizon the most beautiful colors of orange.

Closing my eyes, I started to pray, "Lord, I did it. I stopped myself from bingeing and purging when the desire was incredibly strong. Thank you, Lord, for being with me and giving me the strength. Am I making the right decision, Lord? I am not trying to hurt my parents, but somehow I always manage to do just that. Please help my parents understand why I must move to Texas with Scott. Please help them forgive me for hurting them. Will I have the strength to follow through with everything I am trying to accomplish in my life?"

The strength in my body was dwindling, and I drifted off to sleep for a short time. When I woke up, I was still lying on the ground in the church garden. At first I was disoriented, but soon remembered where I was and what had happened. The chill of the cool evening was causing me to shiver, and I quickly got into my car and drove back to my apartment.

Rushing around the apartment to pick up toys and straighten up a bit, I was feeling nervous about Dad dropping Colby off. He had promised to have him home by six o'clock. It was nearly six, and I was dreading dad's reaction to the news of us moving to Texas with Scott. I knew he wouldn't want to sit down and discuss my decision, but I would probably get the cold shoulder.

Hearing a familiar little boy's voice coming up the stairway, I headed to the front door to let them in.

Opening the door, I was welcomed with a joyful, "Hi, Mom."

I swept him into my arms and gave him a warm hug to go along with his greeting.

"Did you have a good time, sweetheart?" I asked.

"I sure did. Look, I banged up my knee. I wrecked my bike, but I'm okay," he stated trying to act like a tough little boy.

"You sure did. I'm glad you are okay," I replied giving him a motherly kiss on the cheek.

Looking up in the direction of my father, I could tell mom had told him the news. He wouldn't look me in the eye, and there was an uneasiness that could be felt in the room.

Trying to break the ice, I stated, "Hi, Dad."

"Hey, Colby was very good for your mom and I," he stated handing me Colby's overnight bag. He still would not look at me.

"Good, I'm glad he was," I said shutting the door. Handing Colby his bag, I stated, "Why don't you put your bag in your room for me. Thank you."

"Sure, Mom," he replied grabbing the bag and happily skipping down the hallway.

Turning to face my father, I asked, "Dad, can I talk with you?"

"If you want to talk about what your mother has told me, then no. I agree with your mother and have nothing more to say about it. Your mother and I want you to know that the car you are driving needs to be returned to us before you leave for Texas," he stated firmly.

"But I am paying payments on that car to you. I promise I will still make the payments. I thought you wanted to sell that car."

"We do, but just not to you. I will figure up how much you have paid and return that money to you when you return the car. Good-bye," he said walking out the door.

I stood there stunned by his words. The only reason he didn't want to sell it to me now was because I was choosing to work things out with Scott. What would Scott and I do for a vehicle? I reminded myself it was only a material item that could be replaced. It wasn't going to change my mind about moving with Scott to Texas.

"Mom, I'm hungry," said Colby tugging on my shirt.

I was so lost in my thoughts; I'd forgotten that Colby was even home.

"You are? How would you like some cookies and milk before you get a bath and head to bed?"

"That sounds yummy," he stated rubbing his little tummy.

"Come here," I said stretching my arms out to pick him up. "I almost can't pick you up anymore. You know that? You are getting so big," I said giving him a kiss and placing him on the bar stool. "You sit here, and I'll get you some cookies and milk."

"Do I have school tomorrow?" he asked.

"Yes, we both have school. Actually, we have a big day tomorrow," I replied sitting a plate of cookies in front of him.

"What else are we doing?" he asked biting into a cookie.

"We have school in the morning, and then after lunch we are going to the airport in Kansas City to pick up one of my friends."

"Will I get to see big airplanes flying?" he asked with a mouthful of cookie.

"Yes, you'll get to see lots of big planes."

I had decided not to tell Colby that the friend we were picking up at the airport was his father. I was getting nervous about the entire situation. The letter was real; I still had it and read it everyday. After three years of not seeing someone, the reality of actually getting to see them again is almost dreamlike. The letter says he'll be there, but it won't seem real until I can see him. I didn't know if I was handling the situation correctly with Colby or not, but my decision was made. I would say it was a friend until Scott and I felt the time was right to tell him otherwise.

"You must've been hungry. Do you want anything else before a bath?" I asked putting the plate and cup in the kitchen sink.

"No thanks," he replied with a big yawn.

"It looks like you are tired from all your adventures with Grandpa," I said picking him up into my arms.

"I am tired," he replied laying his head on my shoulder.

After bath and a story, Colby went right to sleep. I decided to let him sleep with me tonight. I wanted him close to me. Just having him near gave me a feeling of security and peace. My nerves were on edge this evening. I knew it was from what tomorrow would bring. A lot of different emotions were twirling around in me causing me to be restless most of the night.

I was excited about Scott coming home and the idea of us getting back together. There were issues that scared me though. Would Scott and I be able to work through the issues that caused us to divorce? Scott and I had grown distant from one another. I still wasn't sure why. He came back a different person from Korea. There was an anger and harshness in his voice at times. I hadn't seen this before in him. There were times when he would go for weeks not talking to me. Would it still be that way?

I wanted to give this relationship everything I had to make it work. Could I give it my all yet? I still struggled with my eating disorder, but I had made huge progress in controlling it. My tough journey of ridding myself of this illness was far from over though.

I knew I needed to pray to the one person who was always there for me.

"Lord, please help me sort through the different feelings and thoughts I am having right now. My heart tells me that I need to be at that airport tomorrow and my future is with Scott. I know Scott and I will have many struggles ahead of us. Please help us, Lord, to work through them. I want Colby to know his father and be a part of his life. I know I have a long ways to go before I can say I am free of this terrible illness. I still have so much to learn about you, Lord, but I am learning to trust you with my life. Help me to make the right decision."

The day seemed to be dragging along. I didn't think my morning classes would ever end. The lunch hour finally rolled around, and Colby and I had a quick picnic on the campus lawn by the daycare building.

We were finally on the road heading for the airport, but my insides were shaking so badly that I was having a hard time driving. I kept taking deep breaths and letting them out slowly.

"Look over there, Mom. There's a big plane," he said excitedly.

"I see it. It is big," I replied nervously.

We didn't have much time before his plane would be landing. I had meant to get to the airport earlier, but it took forever for me to decide what to wear. I must've changed clothes five times before deciding on the perfect outfit. It seemed silly to worry about such a minor thing, but when I'm a ball of nerves I have a tendency to do silly things at times.

Parking the car, I hurriedly unhooked Colby from his car seat.

"Come on, sweetie, we need to hurry," I said feeling little butterflies fluttering around in my stomach.

We quickly made it into the airport and found the terminal. His plane would be landing soon.

"You want to watch the airplanes land on the runway?" I asked Colby.

"Sure," he said running over to the large glass wall.

I checked the television monitor to see if his flight was on time. His mother had told me he was flying in from Chicago on a Southwest flight. The monitor showed that his flight would be on time. I was thankful. I didn't know how much more waiting I could handle. I'd already waited three years to see him, and truthfully I thought I might burst if I had to wait much longer.

"Look, Mom, there's a big plane landing," Colby said excitedly.

"I see it."

I noticed it was a Southwest plane. How I hoped it was Scott's plane. I watched it carefully to see which terminal it would pull into. When it actually pulled into our terminal, my heart felt like it had stopped.

"Look. Look how big that plane is," he said jumping up and down.

"I know, Colby. That is my friend's plane. Let's go stand closer to the door so we can watch for him," I said barely able to get the words out.

It seemed to take forever for the passengers to start unloading. Would I even recognize Scott? Would he be in military uniform? I kept studying each male passenger getting off the plane. None of them resembled the Scott I remembered. The passengers coming off the plane were thinning out and yet no Scott.

Tears started filling my eyes. He had to be on this plane. I was getting ready to go ask someone to check the passenger list for his name when Colby said, "Look, Mom, there's a man in a green uniform."

Turning around to face where Colby was pointing, I saw Scott walking our direction. My heart felt like it had stopped, and I couldn't breathe. It was Scott, and he looked as handsome as the day he left.

Bending down next to Colby, I said, "You're right, Colby. That is my friend we came to pick up."

Tears were running down my cheeks. I couldn't have stopped them if I had tried. As Scott got closer to us, Colby grabbed a hold of me and started to tremble.

"Mom...Mom," Colby said shaking my arm.

"What, sweetheart?" I asked.

Whispering into my ear, he said, "I think that is my daddy. That is my daddy."

Looking into Colby's eyes, I replied, "You're right, sweetheart; that is your daddy."

Picking him up into my arms, we both started to cry. When I looked back towards Scott's direction, I noticed he was staring at us. For a moment, we just looked at each other. Tears filled his eyes and slowly made their way down his face. Scott was real, and he was here. How I hoped it wasn't all a dream.

Scott walked over and without a word wrapped his arms around the both of us. It was a hug that will be forever embedded in my mind.

Colby immediately wanted to crawl into his father's arms. I could feel the intense feeling of happiness and joy that filled our little boy. There was no doubt in my mind that I had made the right decision.

After a few minutes of crying tears of joy and happiness, Scott said, "I love you both very much."

"I love you, Daddy," Colby said throwing his arms around his dad's neck.

Looking at me for an answer, Scott asked, "I'm ready to go home now. How about you?"

Smiling, I replied, "Yes, let's go home." Leaning over to give him a kiss on the cheek, I whispered, "I love you too."

EPILOGUE

Who am I? Where do I fit in? What do I want to do with my life? It is common for adolescents to address such questions. As a child enters into their adolescent years, their peers help establish the different values and forms of self-expression they might experiment with. Power struggles between parents and children are normal yet very challenging. As a young adult starts to prepare for life on her own, the separation process from parents can have many challenges.

Looking back at my younger years, I can remember wanting to be my own person. I didn't just want to be somebody's daughter or wife, but I wanted to reach out to complete strangers and make a difference in somebody's life. How was I supposed to accomplish this? Was I being what God created me to be? I didn't have the answers to these questions.

One day while visiting with a priest, he told me that the Lord gives us clues to what He wants us to be by giving each of us unique gifts. To be honest, I struggled for a long time trying to figure out what my gift was. After years of counseling, I discovered some truth behind what my therapist was trying to teach me. My gifts have something to do with the suffering I endured while struggling with my eating disorder and the ability to express my feelings through words.

My knowledge about eating disorders and the emotional pain that goes along with it come from personal experiences. I have heard comments from individuals that eating disorders are about wanting to be thin. It is much more than wanting to be thin or about what you are eating. It had everything to do with what was eating at my heart. Bulimia nervosa became part of my identity, a way to cope with stress in life, and a powerful and dangerous addiction.

There came a point in my life when I knew I had to make a choice. I could either let the eating disorder destroy me, or I could defeat it. It's not easy admitting you have a problem that is hurting you and your loved ones. You have to let go of the bitterness, shame, embarrassment, and anger that builds up inside of you. This is not an easy task to accomplish, and it does take a strong person to admit to their wrongs. The pain can be unbearable at times, but it can also be rewarding. Painful events can give you a deeper appreciation for life and being thankful for what you do have. The pain has shaped me into having compassion and understanding of others who suffer emotionally and, without doubt, made me a stronger person.

What should you do if you think someone you know has an eating disorder? You should try to talk with the person in private without any interruptions. Understand that the person may become defensive and probably will not admit they have a problem. Be open and honest about your concerns by explaining the things you see that concern you. Let them know that they do not have to suffer in silence; there are medical professionals that can help.

If your friend is defensive and denies having a problem, do not have a conflict over who is right or wrong. Try to be a good listener and supportive of their feelings and thoughts. After they have vocalized their feelings, repeat your concerns. Offer your assistance in finding a medical professional that could help identify if there is a problem that needs to be addressed. Be willing to set up an appointment for them, and let them know you are willing to go along for support.

Keep in mind when talking with your friend, you shouldn't place blame or use statements that are degrading. Statements such as, "This is so stupid," or "Your actions are ridiculous," are humiliating. Do not give simple solution statements such as, "Just stop it," or "Just start eating." There is nothing simple about ridding yourself of an eating disorder. It is a tough journey, but from experience I can say a battle well worth fighting.

I have found comfort in writing my thoughts and feelings on paper. It has allowed me to spend time learning more about myself and who I have become. It allows me to reflect on my life, the people I love, and what I hold important. In the beginning, I was a young girl trying to figure out my path in life; now I am a grown woman who understands her path is to reach out and help others.

If I was asked to compose a journal entry to express my thoughts and feelings about my experience, I would write...

> Lord,
>
> How blessed can a person be? Thank you, Lord, for the many blessings you have brought into my life. I know I have so much more to learn in my spiritual journey, but you have gotten my attention. I put my life into your hands, and I trust that you will not forsake me. It brings me comfort to know that you will be there for me when struggles come knocking at my door once again. I have learned that I do not have to suffer alone in silence. You have always been there for me.
>
> I wonder at times what kind of person I might have been if I hadn't experienced the challenges and emotional pain of an eating disorder. You have taught me, Lord, that facing difficult challenges and pain are a part of life. My eating disorder has taken me beyond what was comfortable and secure, allowing me to see the importance of having you in every part of my life. I know now that I shouldn't worry about what I might have been, but what I have become. I am the person I am today because of the lessons you have taught me and the wonderful parents you blessed me with.
>
> Being a parent myself, I can understand how difficult it is to let your children grow up. You don't want to see them suffer or make mistakes. You blessed me with a caring mother and father, and I am very grateful to

them. Even in their own weaknesses, my parents always did what they could for all of us children. I know when I was suffering with my eating disorder I caused a lot of pain for loved ones. Please help them to understand that I am sorry.

Thank you, Lord, for the gifts you have blessed me with. The path you have taken me down is more wonderful than any dream I could've imagined.

Amen.